MOBY DICK

A Play Adapted from
Herman Melville's Novel

by

Mark Lee

© Copyright 2020 by Mark W. Lee

MOBY DICK: A Play Adapted from Herman Melville's Novel by Mark Lee is fully protected under the copyright laws of the United States of America and of all other countries covered by the Pan-American Copyright Convention and the Universal Copyright Convention.

The stage performance rights of this theatrical adaptation are controlled exclusively by the playwright.

This play was written in order to increase awareness and appreciation of a great American novel. Because of that goal the author is making a distinction between "student" productions of this adaptation and "professional" productions.

Student productions of the adaptation are performances produced under the auspices of a school or educational institution. Either no admission or a nominal admission will be charged. Most or all of the performers will be students.

Student productions will not have to pay royalties for a limited amount of performances of the adaptation. However directors and/or teachers in charge of the production must notify the playwright of the production. The full title of the adaptation must be on the performance programs and displayed in all advertisements, posters or promotional materials.

Contact: http://www.markwlee.com/

Professional productions are performances that use professional actors and a creative staff working for pay. These performances can charge admission and will be advertised.

Professional stage performances of this adaptation MOBY DICK will require the permission of the playwright and will require royalties that will reflect the size of the venue. The author will defend the copyright of this adaptation against unauthorized professional productions.

Contact: http://www.markwlee.com/

This edition published by Brook Farm Books
Paperback Edition ISBN: 978-1-947635-34-0
Eboook Edition ISBN: 978-1-947635-35-7

CHARACTER LIST & CASTING SUGGESTIONS

Moby Dick can be staged with 12 actors.

A dozen characters from the novel will be separated into four boats to hunt whales:

1. Ahab, Fedallah and a sailor.
2. Starbuck, Queequeg and Ishmael.
3. Stubb, Tashtego and Pip.
4. Flask, Daggoo and a sailor.

Obviously, a larger cast creates more possibilities. One staging choice is that all actors play multiple roles except for Ishmael and Ahab.

As the play's director and creative team begin to organize a production of Moby Dick, the play's structure will suggest a variety of choices.

The three harpooners act as the play's "Greek chorus." They change the set, hand out props and comment on the action.

Doubling roles allows characters in the New Bedford and Nantucket scenes (Peter Coffin, Father Mapple, etc) to echo characters that appear on the Pequod.

The *Midnight, Forecastle* scene that Melville wrote as a short play can feature the different seamen as described or – with a smaller cast – the singing can be done by Stubb and Flask.

As in the novel, the last third of the play builds dramatic tension when the Pequod encounters a series of ships. Once again, the actors should double roles to portray a variety of different sea captains.

CHARACTERS (in order of appearance)

QUEEQUEG

DAGGOO

TASHTEGO

ISHMAEL

PETER COFFIN

FATHER MAPPLE

THE CONGREGATION OF THE WHALEMAN'S CHAPEL

CAPTAIN PELEG

CAPTAIN BILDAD

EJIJAH

THE PEQUOD'S CREW

STARBUCK

STUBB

FLASK

PIP

AHAB

NANTUCKET SAILOR

ENGLISH SAILOR

SPANISH SAILOR

MALTESE SAILOR

FEDALLAH

MANILLA SAILOR

GURNSEYMAN

FRENCH CAPTAIN

CAPTAIN BOOMER

DR. BUNGER

CARPENTER

CAPTAIN GARDINER

CAPTAIN OF THE DELIGHT

A FEW THOUGHTS ON CASTING

"In thoroughfares nigh the docks, any considerable seaport will frequently offer to view the queerest looking nondescripts from foreign parts. Even in Broadway and Chestnut streets, Mediterranean mariners will sometimes jostle the affrighted ladies. Regent street is not unknown to Lascars and Malays; and at Bombay, in the Apollo Green, live Yankees have often scared the natives." - Chapter VI

"As for the residue of the Pequod's company, be it said, that at the present day not one in two of the many thousand men before the mast employed in the American whale fishery, are Americans born, though nearly all the officers are." – Chapter XXVII

***

As Melville learned during his five years at sea, a typical whaling ship crew was a dramatically heterogeneous group of people. If the Pequod is a floating symbol of our world, then the actors in a production of *Moby Dick* should reflect the widest possible spectrum of humanity.

ACT I

An open stage dominated by the skeleton of a whale. The framework of bones resembles the structure of a ship.

The skeleton is placed diagonally so that the whale's jaws are downstage left. Ropes hang from the ceiling, allowing the actors to climb to the top of the backbone.

A mast with a rope ladder leading to a crow's nest is downstage right. An elevated platform within the audience is used as the deck of other ships that encounter the Pequod.

The three harpooners -- Queequeg, Daggoo, and Tashtego -- wear masks that cover the top half of the face. The masks are similar to the ritual disguises found in the Polynesian, African, and Native American cultures.

Music. Lights up on Queequeg standing on the whale's backbone.

          QUEEQUEG
And god created great whales.

Daggoo appears in the whale's jaws.

          DAGGOO
The great Leviathan that maketh the seas to seethe like a boiling pan.

Tashtego slides down a rope.

          TASHTEGO
Hugest of living creatures, in the deep
Stretched like a promontory, sleeps or swims
And seems a moving land; and in his gills
Draws in, and at his breath spouts out a sea.

          QUEEQUEG
It is...a mammiferous animal without hind feet.

          DAGGOO
It is...the largest animal in all creation.

> **TASHTEGO**
> It is...a shimmering sign of the beauty and terror of God.

Music. Ishmael enters through the ribs of the whale.

> **ISHMAEL**
> Call me Ishmael. Some years ago... never mind how long precisely... having little or no money in my purse, and nothing particular to interest me on shore, I thought I would sail about a little and see the watery part of the world.

He picks up a carpet bag.

> **ISHMAEL**
> So I stuffed a shirt or two in my old carpet-bag, tucked it under my arm, and started for the whaling town of Nantucket. Arriving in New Bedford on a Saturday night, I I walked through the dark streets until I found The Spouter Inn... Peter Coffin, Proprietor.

Peter Coffin enters carrying a bench. He sets down the bench and notices Ishmael.

> **ISHMAEL**
> Landlord...I have a desire to be accommodated with a room.

> **COFFIN**
> House is full. All beds taken.

> **ISHMAEL**
> The packet has already sailed for Nantucket. I need a place to spend the night.

> **COFFIN**
> Not my problem, is it? Away with you!

> **ISHMAEL**
> I could pay...extra.

> **COFFIN**
> Yes, well...perhaps we could find something. You haint no objections to sharing a harpooner's blanket, have you?

                    ISHMAEL
          Well, I've never liked to sleep two
          in a bed, but if there is no other
          place for me and if this harpooner
          is not decidedly objectionable...

Coffin forces Ishmael to sit on the bench.

                    COFFIN
          All right. Stop your jabberin' and
          take a seat. Supper will be ready
          directly.

                    ISHMAEL
          Is the harpooner at the inn?

                    COFFIN
          He'll be here before long.

Tashtego hands Coffin a plate of bread and cheese and the
innkeeper serves the food.

                    ISHMAEL
          What sort of person is he?

                    COFFIN
          Dark complexioned chap. He eats
          nothing but steaks and likes 'em
          rare.

                    ISHMAEL
          Does he always keep such late
          hours? It's almost midnight.

                    COFFIN
          No. Generally, he's an early bird...
          airley to bed and airley to rise...
          but tonight he's engaged in selling
          his head.

                    ISHMAEL
          I beg your pardon?

                    COFFIN
          Head. Got a head. Trying to sell it.

                    ISHMAEL
          What sort of a bamboozingly story
          is this you're telling me? Do
          you mean to say this harpooner is
          peddling his head around town?

                    COFFIN
          Yes. I told him he couldn't sell it
          here. The market's overstocked.

                    ISHMAEL
          With what?

                    COFFIN
          With heads to be sure. Ain't there
          too many heads in the world?

Daggoo hands Coffin a blanket.

                    ISHMAEL
          You better stop spinning this yarn
          to me. I'm not green.

                    COFFIN
          Maybe not. But you'll be done <u>brown</u>
          if that ere harpooner hears you
          slandering his head.

Ishmael puts down the plate and jumps up.

                    ISHMAEL
          Landlord! If you have good evidence
          that this harpooner is stark mad
          and yet are trying to induce me to
          sleep with this madman...you are
          thereby rendering yourself liable
          to criminal prosecution!

                    COFFIN
          Easy now. I don't want trouble.

Coffin picks up Ishmael's carpet bag and crosses the stage to
the whale's mouth. He kneels, pulls up a section of the floor
and uses chunks of wood to elevate it at a 45 degree angle.
(Note: this "bed" should be framed by the jaws of the whale)

                    COFFIN
          This here harpooner has just
          arrived from the South Seas where
          he bought up a lot of 'balmed New
          Zealand heads...great curios, you
          know...and he's sold all of 'em but
          one. And that one he's trying to
          sell tonight, cause tomorrow's
          Sunday, and it wouldn't do to be
          sellin' human heads when folks is
          goin' to church.

                    ISHMAEL
          He...he's a dangerous man.

                    COFFIN
          He pays reg'lar.

Coffin places the blanket on the bed.

                    COFFIN
          Come on. Get beneath the covers.
          It's a nice bed.

Wary, Ishmael slips beneath the blanket.

                    COFFIN
          Sal and me slept in that ere bed
          the night we were spliced. There's
          plenty room for two to kick about
          in it.

                    ISHMAEL
          Landlord, I...

                    COFFIN
          Why, afore we gave it up, Sal used
          to put our Sam and little Johnny at
          the foot of it.

                    ISHMAEL
          All I want to know is...

                    COFFIN
          But I got a dreaming and sprawling
          about one night, and somehow, Sam
          got pitched on the floor and came
          near to breaking his arm.

                    ISHMAEL
          When is he going to...

                    COFFIN
          Night.

Coffin exits. Daggoo and Tashtego sit on top of the whale's
jaws -- looking down at the bed.

                    ISHMAEL
          I slid off into a light doze, then
          a stranger entered...

Queequeg steps into the light. He lights a pipe made from a
tomahawk, then removes his boots and hat.

                    DAGGOO
          His face was of a dark, purplish,
          yellow color, here and there stuck
          over with huge blackish looking
          squares.

                    TASHTEGO
          There was no hair on his head, but
          a small scalpknot twisted up on his
          forehead.

                    DAGGOO
          He lit a tomahawk, puffed out great
          clouds of tobacco smoke and...

Queequeg sits down on the bed while Ishmael tries to hide
beneath the blanket. Queequeg starts to feel Ishmael's body.

                    QUEEQUEG
          Ummm...

                    ISHMAEL
          Good day. I mean, good evening.
          Call me...Call me...

                    QUEEQUEG
          Ummmm...

                    ISHMAEL
          Ishmael. Yes. I was traveling to
          Nantucket, but the packet boat had
          already sailed and...

Queequeg pulls Ishmael up by his hair.

                    QUEEQUEG
          Who the devil you? Why you in my
          bed?

                    ISHMAEL
          Landlord! For God's sake! Peter
          Coffin! Help!

Coffin enters wearing a nightgown and carrying a candle.

                    COFFIN
          Don't be afraid now. Queequeg here
          wouldn't harm a hair of your head.

                    ISHMAEL
          Why didn't you tell me that this
          man's a cannibal!

                    COFFIN
          Didn't I tell you, he was peddlin'
          heads around town?
                    (turns to Queequeg)
          Queequeg, look here. You sabbee me.
          I sabbee you. This man sleepe you.
          Ahhh...sabbee?

                    QUEEQUEG
          Me sabbee plenty.

He crawls beneath the blanket and turns to Ishmael.

                    QUEEQUEG
          You sleep.

                    COFFIN
          Go on. Better a sober cannibal than
          a drunken Christian.

                    ISHMAEL
          Just...just tell him to get rid of
          his tomahawk there, or pipe, or
          whatever you call it.

                    COFFIN
          Come on, Queequeg. Hand it over. I
          ain't insured.

Queequeg hesitates, then hands the pipe to Coffin. Cautiously, Ishmael gets into bed.

                    ISHMAEL
          Good night, landlord. You...you may go.

Coffin smiles and exits. Daggoo and Tashtego disappear.

                    ISHMAEL
          I turned in, and never slept better
          in my life.

Queequeg reaches up and pulls Ishmael down onto the bed.

                    ISHMAEL
          Upon waking next morning about
          daylight, I found Queequeg's arm
          thrown over me in the most loving
          and affectionate manner. You had
          almost thought I had been his wife.

Ishmael tries to get up, but Queequeg hugs him even closer.

                    ISHMAEL
          Queequeg...Ahhh, Mr. Queequeg. If
          don't mind.
                    (pushes the arm)
          If you could just move your arm
          over here and ahhh...
                    (no response)
          Queequeg, in the name of goodness!
          Wake up!

Queequeg wakes up and rolls out of bed.

                    ISHMAEL
          Of course if you'd like to sleep a
          little longer, that's all right
          with me.

                    QUEEQUEG
          Hat.

                    ISHMAEL
          Yes. Yes. Your hat. Right here.

Ishmael gives Queequeg his hat.

                    QUEEQUEG
          Boots.

                    ISHMAEL
          Of course. Hats lead to boots.
          Boots lead to hats. It's logical.

He hands Queequeg his boots.

                    QUEEQUEG
          Blanket.

                    ISHMAEL
          Ahhh, yes...blanket. Here you go.

Queequeg squats down, puts the blanket over his head, and moves beneath it.

                    ISHMAEL
          Is everything all right, Queequeg?
          Can I help you with your...

Queequeg pulls off the blanket. He's wearing his boots.

                    ISHMAEL
          Good. Very good. You put those
          boots on very...privately.

Queequeg picks up his harpoon. Intimidated, Ishmael backs away.

                    ISHMAEL
          I just wanted to mention that I've
          never said anything insulting about
          cannibals. Although the idea of
          eating such a dinner does not
          appeal to me personally, one man's
          meat is another man's...

Queequeg whets the harpoon blade on his boot, peers into a "mirror" and begins to shave. Ishmael stands beside him and looks at the mirror.

                    ISHMAEL
          Shave. You're using that to shave.

                    QUEEQUEG
Sharp.

                    ISHMAEL
I'm sure it is. My god, this is
using Rogers's best cutlery with a
vengeance.

                    QUEEQUEG
            (brandishes harpoon)
Call me...Queequeg. Good morning.

Queequeg exits.

                    ISHMAEL
And with that, he marched out of
the room, sporting his harpoon like
a marshal's baton. I myself
dressed, ate breakfast, then
sallied out for a stroll through
the streets of New Bedford.

Music. Lights up. All the characters except Arab move across
the stage. Ishmael is almost knocked over by a man pushing a
wheelbarrow. He stares at Daggoo and Tashtego as they walk by
carrying their harpoons.

The music fades. A spotlight shines on the mast. People carry
on benches and assemble for a sermon.

                    ISHMAEL
Feeling the need for spiritual
comfort, I entered the Whaleman's
Chapel. The chaplain had not
arrived; and yet silent islands of
women and men sat steadfastly
eyeing several marble tables on
either side of the pulpit.

A young woman stands up.

                    WOMAN #1
Sacred to the memory of John Talbot
who, at the age of 18, was lost
overboard near the Isle of Desolation.

A woman stands.

                    WOMAN #2
Sacred to the memory of Captain
Ezekiel Hardy who was killed by a
whale off the coast of Japan.

Captain Peleg stands.

                    PELEG
          Sacred to the memory of Robert
          Long, Willis Ellery, Nathan...

Father Mapple strides into the chapel.

                    MAPPLE
          Starboard gangway, there! Side away
          to larboard! Larboard gangway to
          starboard! Midship! Midships!

He walks over to the mast and starts to climb the rope ladder
to the crow's nest.

                    MAPPLE
          Beloved shipmates, they call me
          Mapple...Father Mapple. I'm the
          pilot of this frail craft floating
          through a ocean of sinners. Today,
          we're going to clinch the last
          verse of the first chapter of
          Jonah: "And God had prepared a
          great fish to swallow up Jonah."

He reaches the crow's nest and looks down at his congregation.

                    MAPPLE
          So, who was this Jonah...son of
          Amittai? God ask him to preach to
          Nineveh and he refused. Not only
          did he commit the sin of disobedience,
          but he also thought that he could
          flee from God. That a ship made by
          men could carry him to a country
          where God does not reign.
               (shakes his head)
          Look at him...sulking about the
          wharves of Joppa, seeking a ship
          that's bound for Tarshish. How
          plainly he's a fugitive! No
          baggage! No friends to accompany
          him to the wharf with their adieux.
          When, after a dodging search, he
          finds the Tarshish ship...the crew
          whispers to each other.
               (a sailor's voice)
          "Look at him, Jack; I bet he's
          robbed a widow."
               (another voice)
          "No. I bet he's the adulterer that
          broke out of jail in old Gomorrah."
          Meanwhile, Jonah's down in the
          cabin where the Captain's busy
          making out papers for the Customs.
                              (MORE)

                    MAPPLE
                (Captain's voice)
    "Who's there?" asks the Captain and
    Oh! How that harmless question
    mangles Jonah.
                (Jonah's voice)
    "I...I seek passage in this ship to
    Tarshish. How soon sail ye, sir?"
    The Captain eyes him intently. He
    knows something's not right.
                (Captain's voice)
    "We sail soon enough for any honest
    man that goes a passenger." Jonah
    shivers, but he pays his fare...
    thrice the usual sum...then tries
    to lock himself up in his stateroom.
    The air is close. The ceiling
    almost resting on his forehead. A
    swinging lamp oscillates back and
    forth as Jonah's tormented eyes
    roll about the place and...then...
    he sleeps. The tide comes up. The
    ship casts off her cables and
    glides off to sea. But the sea
    rebels. It will not bear the wicked
    burden. A dreadful storm comes up
    and Jonah stumbles onto the deck.
    Wave after wave leaps into the
    ship...the rearing bowsprit
    pointing high upward, but soon beat
    downward again towards the deep.
    The crew turns towards Jonah and
    mob him with their questions:
                (sailor's voice)
    "You! What is your country! Who are
    your people!"
                (Jonah's voice)
    "I...I'm a Hebrew," cries Jonah. "I
    fear the Lord, the God of Heaven, who
    hath made the sea and dry land." At
    first, the crew shows pity, but
    when the gale howls louder the
    fugitive is taken up as an anchor
    and dropped into the sea. He goes
    down...down in the whirling heart
    of such a masterless commotion that
    he scarce heeds the moment when he
    drops seething into the yawning
    jaws awaiting him.

Mapple pauses and studies the congregation.

MAPPLE
Shipmates, God has laid but one
hand upon you. Both his hands press
on me. God's wanted Jonah to preach
Truth to the face of Falsehood. Woe
to that pilot of the Living God who
refuses this command. Oh, Father! I
have striven to be Thine, more than
to be this world's, or mine own.
Yet this is nothing. I leave eternity
to Thee. Let us give praise...

Mapple bows his head --- ending the sermon. Music. The congregation rises and sings while Ishmael crosses the stage to the skeleton.

CONGREGATION
The ribs and terrors in the whale,
Arched over me a dismal gloom,
While all God's sun-lit waves rolled by,
And lift me deepening down to doom.

In black distress, I called my God,
When I could scarce believe him mine,
He bowed his ear to my complaints --
No more the whale did me confine.

My song for ever shall record
That terrible, that joyful hour
I gave the glory to my God,
His all the mercy and the power.

Mapple and the congregation exit. Queequeg sits on a bench counting the pages in a large book. Ishmael approaches him.

ISHMAEL
Hello, Queequeg. What are you
reading?

QUEEQUEG
47, 48, 48, 50...
  (astonished)
Ummmm.

ISHMAEL
Oh, you're counting pages. Well,
that's fun too.

Queequeg hands the book to Ishmael.

QUEEQUEG
What is book?

ISHMAEL
Pilgrim's Progress by John Bunyan. It's about a journey a man takes from a land of destruction to the Celestial City. I guess we're all taking that journey although it's easy to get lost on the way.

QUEEQUEG
You talk.

ISHMAEL
Yes, I guess I do. I was a schoolmaster for several years and the one thing schoolmasters like to do is to talk and talk and...

QUEEQUEG
Friends?

ISHMAEL
You and I? Well, we don't really know each other, Queequeg. I mean, we've slept together...that is... we've spent the night in the same bed...that is...

QUEEQUEG
Friends.

ISHMAEL
Well, I...why not? I don't mind a pagan friend. Let me tell you something, Queequeg, Christian kindness is often just a hollow courtesy.

QUEEQUEG
Forever.

ISHMAEL
Friends forever? Yes. That's a true friend, isn't it?

Queequeg touches his own forehead, then touches Ishmael's head.

ISHMAEL
Forever.

Music. Queequeg removes his mask and gives it to Ishmael.

ISHMAEL
That night, Queequeg and I lay in bed and shared his pipe and he told about his native land.

Sound of a drum. Queequeg moves through the ribs of the whale.

> QUEEQUEG
> I was a native of Kokovoko, an island not down on any map. My father was a High Chief, a King. And on my maternal side I was bound to wives of unconquerable warriors. I was a prince of the island, and yet in my ambitious soul lurked a strong desire to see something more of Christendom than a specimen whaler or two.

Queequeg climbs up a rope to the top of the whale.

> QUEEQUEG
> A Sag Harbor ship visited my father's bay and I sought passage to Christian lands. Alone in my canoe, I paddled off to a distant strait and when the ship glided by I darted out, climbed up her chains, and grappled a ring-bolt on the deck...swearing not to let go until I was accepted by the captain.

Queequeg slides down a rope and returns to Ishmael.

> QUEEQUEG
> They made me a harpooner...that length of barbed iron becoming my scepter. At first, I tried to learn from the Christians, but gradually I discovered that they were more miserable and wicked than all my father's heathens. Thought I, it's a wicked world in all meridians; I'll die a pagan.

He takes the mask from Ishmael.

> QUEEQUEG
> And yet I had to live among them. And wear their clothes. And talk their gibberish...

Queequeg puts on the mask and, once again, becomes "the savage." He sits down on the bench next to Ishmael.

> QUEEQUEG
> You. Me. Kill whales.

ISHMAEL
Yes. That was my plan.

Queequeg picks up his bag and harpoon.

QUEEQUEG
We go to Nantucket. You find ship.

ISHMAEL
I'm not really an expert at this, Queequeg. Perhaps you could...

QUEEQUEG
You find ship.

Music. Tashtego gives Ishmael his carpet bag.

ISHMAEL
And so we both took a packet schooner to Nantucket: that lonely village built on a elbow of sand. We found three whaling ships there...all of them up for three-year voyages.

Ishmael guides Queequeg across the stage.

ISHMAEL
There's a ship, Queequeg. It's called the Devil-Dam. Good God. Who thought of that name? Not a good omen there.

He pulls Queequeg in the opposite direction.

ISHMAEL
There's another one. The...the Tit-bit. "The Tit-bit?" I'm sorry, but I can't see spending three years on something called the Tit-bit. Why don't we just...

Ishmael walks towards the skeleton. Queequeg remains in the same position and leans on his harpoon.

ISHMAEL
The Pequod. Yes. The Pequod. That's our ship.

Daggoo and Tashtego lower a strip of canvas over two of the whale ribs so that it forms a little shelter inside the skeleton. Captain Peleg sits on a chair inside the shelter as Ishmael approaches him.

                    DAGGOO
          She was a cannibal of a craft,
          tricking herself forth in the
          chased bones of her enemies.

                    TASHTEGO
          Her bulwarks were garnished with
          the teeth of a Sperm whale while
          her tiller was carved from the
          lower jaw of this hereditary foe.

Ishmael approaches Captain Peleg.

                    ISHMAEL
          Ahhh, excuse me...are you the
          Captain of the Pequod?

                    PELEG
          Supposing it be the Captain of the
          Pequod. What dost thou want of him?

                    ISHMAEL
          I was thinking of shipping.

                    PELEG
          Dost you know anything about
          whaling? I dare you you don't, eh?

                    ISHMAEL
          Nothing, sir. But I have no doubt I
          shall soon learn. I've been on
          several voyages in the merchant
          service, and I think that...

Peleg storms out of the wigwam, advancing towards Ishmael.

                    PELEG
          Merchant service be damned! I'll
          kick you in the stern if you ever
          mention those words to me again.
          Art thou the man to pitch a harpoon
          down a live whale's throat, and
          then jump after it? Answer, quick!

                    ISHMAEL
          I am, sir, if it should be
          positively indispensable to do so.

                    PELEG
          Don't lie to me, young man! What
          makes you want to go a whaling, eh?
          It looks a little suspicious, eh?
          Hast thou been a pirate? Dodst thou
          think of murdering the officers
          when thou gets to sea?

                    ISHMAEL
          Yes...I...I mean, no sir. I want to
          see what whaling is. I want to see
          the world.

                    PELEG
          "See the world?" You want to "see
          the world?"

He grabs Ishmael by the collar and drags him downstage. Both
men are pressed against one of the ribs, staring downstage.

                    PELEG
          Take a look, boy. And tell me what
          you see out there.

                    ISHMAEL
          Nothing but water, sir.
          Considerable water.

                    PELEG
          That's all you're going to see on a
          whaling trip! For three years!

Ishmael pulls away from Peleg.

                    ISHMAEL
          I _have_ been in the merchant service...

                    PELEG
          Don't aggravate me!

                    ISHMAEL
          I'm not trying to...

                    PELEG
          Have you seen Ahab? The Captain of
          the Pequod?

                    ISHMAEL
          I thought you were the Captain, sir.

                    PELEG
          I'm Peleg. Captain Bildad and I are
          part owners of this ship. If you
          saw Ahab, you'd remember him. He
          only has one leg.

                    ISHMAEL
          Was the other one lost by a whale?

                    PELEG
          It was devoured! Chewed up!
          Crunched by the monstrousest
          parmecetty that ever...

Captain Bildad, a stern-looking Quaker, steps from the ribs
of the whale carrying a large ledger and a stool

                    BILDAD
          That's enough, Peleg. Who is this
          young man?

                    PELEG
          He says he's a sailor, Captain
          Bildad. Says he wants to ship.

                    BILDAD
          Dodst thee?
                    (Ishmael hesitates)
          DODST THEE?

                    ISHMAEL
          I...I dodst.

Bildad sits down on the stool and opens the ledger.

                    BILDAD
          Name?

                    ISHMAEL
          Ishmael.

                    BILDAD
          Genesis. Chapter 21. The son of
          Abraham and a Egyptian slave.

                    ISHMAEL
          That was before my time, Captain.

                    BILDAD
          Cast out into the wilderness.
          Wandering through the desert...

                    ISHMAEL
          At least, I'm not called "Ahab." Wasn't
          he one of the wicked kings in the Bible?
          Didn't the dogs lick his blood?

                    BILDAD
          PELEG!

Peleg grabs Ishmael and drags him away from Bildad.

                    PELEG
          Listen, to me, lad. Never say that
          on board the Pequod. Never say it
          anywhere. Captain Ahab did not name
          himself. 'Twas a foolish, ignorant
          whim of his widowed mother who died
          when he was only twelvemonth old.

ISHMAEL
Yes, but...

PELEG
Ahab's above the common. He's been in colleges, as well as 'mong the cannibals. He's a grand, ungodly, godlike man, Captain Ahab. Doesn't speak much. But when he does, you may well listen.

ISHMAEL
I was only saying that...

PELEG
And I'm saying that no one should wrong Captain Ahab because he happens to have a wicked name. He has a wife...not three voyages wedded...and little boy. Hold ye then that Ahab has his humanities! Agreed?

ISHMAEL
Where is Captain Ahab? If you don't mind me asking.

BILDAD
Sick.

Peleg spins Ishmael around and drags him back to Bildad.

PELEG
...But getting better. So sign up! Sign your name in the ledger.

ISHMAEL
We haven't mentioned wages.

BILDAD
I'll give you a lay of 777. If the boat earns that many dollars, you get to keep...one of them.

ISHMAEL
For three years labor?

PELEG
Put him down for a three hundredth lay, Bildad.

BILDAD
Thou must consider our duty to the widows and orphans who own this ship.

PELEG
Blast the widows and the orphans,
too! Sign up, boy! Sign up!

Bildad hands Ishmael a quill with a steel point and he signs
his name in the ledger. Queequeg crosses the stage.

ISHMAEL
I have a friend with me who wants
to ship, too.

PELEG
Fetch him along. We'll take a look
at him.

Queequeg slams the butt of his harpoon on the floor. The two
Captains look startled.

ISHMAEL
This is Queequeg.

PELEG
He's an impressive specimen...of
something.

BILDAD
He's got to have papers.

ISHMAEL
"Papers?"

BILDAD
He must show that he's converted.
    (confronts Queequeg)
You! Son of darkness! Art thou
present in communion at any
Christian church?

QUEEQUEG
Ummmmm.

ISHMAEL
He's...he's a member of the First
Congregational Church.

BILDAD
Do tell, now. Is this Philistine a
regular member of Deacon Deuteronomy's
meeting? I never saw him going
there, and I pass it every Lord's day.

PELEG
He certainly hasn't been baptized
or it would have washed some of
that devil's blue out of his face.

                    BILDAD
               (to Ishmael)
          Are thou skylarking with me?
          Explain thyself, young Hittite.

                    ISHMAEL
          I mean, sir, that he's a member of
          the great and everlasting First
          Congregation of this whole worshipping
          world. We all belong to that. Don't we?

                    PELEG
          Young man, you'd better ship for a
          missionary. I never heard a better sermon.
               (approaching Queequeg)
          By the great anchor, what a harpoon
          he's got there! I say, Quohog, or
          whatever your name is, did you every
          stand at the head of a whale boat?

Holding the harpoon, Queequeg climbs up the mast.

                    QUEEQUEG
          Captain, you see him small drop tar
          on water dere? Spose him one whale
          eye. Well, den...

He throws the harpoon. Tashtego and Daggoo carry the weapon through the air.

                    DAGGOO
          And taking sharp aim at it, he
          darted the iron right over old
          Bildad's broad brim...

                    TASHTEGO
          And struck the glistening tar spot
          out of sight.

Queequeg slides down the mast rope and approaches the two captains.

                    QUEEQUEG
          Spos-ee him whale eye. Dad whale dead.

                    PELEG
          Quick, Bildad! Get the ship's papers!
          We must have Hedgehog there, I mean
          Quohog, in one of our boats!

Music. Queequeg signs the ledger. Peleg and Bildad exit as Ishmael and Queequeg cross the stage.

                    ISHMAEL
          And so, my friend signed his mark
          and was soon enrolled among the
          same ship's company to which I
          myself belonged. Together, we left
          the Pequod and were sauntering away
          from the water when...

Elijah, a man with a crippled arm, peers from the jaws of the whale.

                    ELIJAH
          Brethren, have you joined that ship?

                    ISHMAEL
          You mean the Pequod? Yes, we have
          just signed the articles.

Elijah slowly approaches them.

                    ELIJAH
          Anything down there about your souls?

                    ISHMAEL
          About what?

                    ELIJAH
          Oh, perhaps you haven't got any.
          No matter. A soul's a sort of fifth
          wheel to a wagon for some men.

                    ISHMAEL
          What are you jabbering about?

                    ELIJAH
          Ahab's got enough, though, to make up
          for all deficiencies.

                    ISHMAEL
          Queequeg, let's go. This fellow has
          broken loose from somewhere.

                    ELIJAH
          You haven't seen Old Thunder. Have
          you? Ahab. Captain of the Pequod.

                    ISHMAEL
          They say he's sick, but getting better.

                    ELIJAH
          Yes. Of course. When Captain Ahab
          is all right, then this left arm of
          mine will be all right. Not before.

ISHMAEL
I'm sure he's a very good whale hunter.

ELIJAH
That's true. True enough. But have you heard about the leg? How he lost it? I'm sure you have. Everyone knows...almost. That he has only one leg and that a whale took the other.

ISHMAEL
We know all about it.

ELIJAH
All about it? Sure you do? All?

Queequeg points his harpoon at Elijah's face.

QUEEQUEG
Lookee here! You go 'way!

Elijah raises his hands and retreats.

ELIJAH
Of course. If that's what you wish. You've shipped, have you? Well, what's signed is signed. And what's to be, will be. And then again, perhaps it won't be, after all.

ISHMAEL
If there's some secret you want to tell us...out with it! Or go away.

ELIJAH
I'll go away then, if that pleases you. It's fixed and arranged already and I suppose some sailors must go with him. Morning to you, shipmates. Morning. I'm sorry I stopped you.

ISHMAEL
If you're only trying to bamboozle us, you're mistaken in your game.

ELIJAH
I like to hear a chap talk up that way. You're just the man for Ahab... the likes of you. Morning.

ISHMAEL
Who the blazes are you? What's your name?

Elijah stands in the jaws of the whale.

ELIJAH
I'm called Elijah. Elijah. May God pity you...

Elijah exits. Ishmael looks disturbed, then he glances at Queequeg.

QUEEQUEG
Ummmmmm.

ISHMAEL
That's what I say, Queequeg. With all my heart.

He turns and shouts after Elijah.

ISHMAEL
Humbug! You're a humbug! That's all!

Music. The entire crew -- except Ahab --appear on stage. They pull ropes and carry on cargo while Peleg and Bildad give orders.

ISHMAEL
A day or two passed, and then there was great activity aboard the Pequod. The crew carried on their chests as well as spare boats, spare lines and harpoons, spare everything, almost, but a spare Captain and a duplicate ship.

Peleg speaks to Starbuck, the First Mate.

PELEG
Aft there, ye sons of bachelors! Mr. Starbuck, drive 'em aft!

BILDAD
No, need of profane words, however great the hurry.

PELEG
And then what'll I do, Bildad? Throw flowers at their feet?

Ishmael and the other men start to pull a rope.

>   PELEG
> Jump, you blocks of wood! Blood and
> thunder! Jump, I say!
>   (raises fist)
> You! Ishmael! Is that the way they
> heave in the merchant service?
> Spring, thou sheep-head, spring,
> and break thy backbone.
>   (to Queequeg)
> Why don't you spring! Quohag!
> Spring, all of ye. And spring
> your eyes out!
>
>   BILDAD
> That's enough, Captain Peleg. The
> sailboat's waiting. We're going
> back to a nice warm fire while
> they're sailing around the world.

The two men climb over the edge of the stage, then walk out of the theatre. Bildad lags behind.

>   PELEG
> Luck to ye, men. Good luck to ye
> all. Three years from now, I'll
> have a hot supper smoking for ye in
> old Nantucket. Hurrah and away!
>
>   BILDAD
> God bless ye, and have ye in His
> holy keeping, men. I hope ye'll
> have fine weather now, so that
> Captain Ahab may soon be moving
> among ye. Don't whale it too much
> on the Lord's days, but don't miss
> a fair chance either, that's
> rejecting Heaven's good gifts. If
> you touch at the islands, beware of
> fornication. Goodbye! Goodbye!
> Don't keep that cheese too long
> down in the hold. It'll spoil. Be
> careful with the butter...twenty
> cents a pound it was...and mind ye,
> if...

Peleg grabs Bildad and pulls him away.

>   PELEG
> Come, Bildad! Stop palavering! Away!
>
>   QUEEQUEG
> Ship and boat diverged...
>
>   DAGGOO
> A screaming gull flew overhead...

                    TASHTEGO
          And the Pequod plunged like fate
          into the lone Atlantic.

Music. The lights change. Each member of the crew stands alone. Ishmael walks past them to the mast.

                    ISHMAEL
          On that first day, I met the rest
          of the crew. They were from all
          parts of the world...from every
          race and nationality...and yet a
          great many of them had been born on
          an island. Isolatoes, I call such,
          not acknowledging the common
          continent of men, but each Isolato
          living on a separate continent of
          his own.

Ishmael starts to coil a rope. Starbuck approaches him.

                    STARBUCK
          Ishmael...is that your name?

                    ISHMAEL
          Yes, sir. And who might I be
          talking to, sir?

                    STARBUCK
          Starbuck. First mate. You're going
          to be pulling an oar in my whale
          boat.

                    ISHMAEL
          I'll try to do my best, sir.

                    STARBUCK
          "Your best" is sufficient when
          we're standing on dry land. In a
          whale boat our lives are joined
          together. It's a mutual, joint-stock
          world, in all meridians. The
          cannibals helping the Christians.

                    ISHMAEL
          Don't worry about me, Mr. Starbuck.
          When I see a whale, I'll shake my
          fist and spit in his eye.

                    STARBUCK
          You're not frightened of a beast
          that can crush you with one flip of
          his tail?

ISHMAEL
No, sir! Not me!

STARBUCK
Then you can stay here and scrub the deck. I'll have no man on my boat who's not afraid of the whale.

Starbuck starts to walk away.

ISHMAEL
I am afraid, sir. A little. More than little.

STARBUCK
I see.

ISHMAEL
I just thought that whalers are supposed to be fearless.

STARBUCK
An utterly fearless man is more dangerous than a coward. Courage is just a staple on this ship...like beef and bread...not foolishly wasted. We're here to kill whales for our living; and not to be killed by them.

ISHMAEL
I'll agree to that, Mr. Starbuck.

STARBUCK
Good. Good man.

Stubb enters, puffing on his pipe.

STUBB
What are saying to that lubber, Mr. Starbuck? He's a dry-dock sailor if I'm not mistaken.

STARBUCK
Find out for yourself, Mr. Stubb.

STUBB
Indeed I will. Stubb can smell a fool ten paces away.

Stubb approaches Ishmael and pretends to sniff him.

STUBB
I smell parlors and pulpits and a pinch of chalk dust. None of the stench of a whaling ship.

　　　　　　　　　　ISHMAEL
　　　　Perhaps not at this point of the
　　　　voyage, Mr. Stubb. But I plan to be
　　　　diligent.

　　　　　　　　　　STUBB
　　　　"Diligent." Now, that's a word to
　　　　remember when the whale's smashing
　　　　your boat into toothpicks.

　　　　　　　　　　ISHMAEL
　　　　Mr. Starbuck said that we should
　　　　afraid of the whale. That is...
　　　　properly cautious.

　　　　　　　　　　STUBB
　　　　That's Starbuck's way and he's the
　　　　first mate. I'm the second mate.
　　　　Second don't argue with the first.
　　　　But in _my_ boat we don't worry
　　　　about about being cautious. The
　　　　whole thing's a joke so you might
　　　　as well laugh.

　　　　　　　　　　ISHMAEL
　　　　But the whales can kill you.

　　　　　　　　　　STUBB
　　　　They haven't killed _me_. Not yet.

Stubb crosses the stage and leans against the jaws of the whale.

　　　　　　　　　　STUBB
　　　　The jaws of death are just another
　　　　easy chair as far as I can
　　　　understand. You might as well sit
　　　　down, get comfortable, and see what
　　　　happens.

He lights a match on the whale's jaw bone.

　　　　　　　　　　ISHMAEL
　　　　Mr. Stubb, would you please tell me
　　　　what you mix into your rum? I'll
　　　　drink a barrel of that elixir if it
　　　　makes me half as brave as you.

　　　　　　　　　　STUBB
　　　　It's nothing I drink or eat. It's
　　　　the pipe. Before I pull on my
　　　　trousers, I put this pipe in my mouth.

Stubb walks over to Ishmael and holds up his short black pipe.

STUBB
You see, in the time of cholera, people go about holding camphorated handkerchiefs over their mouths to ward off against death. I've got my pipe and the smoke keeps all the bad thoughts from seeping into my skull.

ISHMAEL
Amazing.

Flask walks across the deck.

STUBB
It's science. That's what it is. Now if you want to meet a truly brave man talk to Mr. Flask...the third mate. As far as he's concerned, the whale's just a sort of magnified mouse.

Flask approaches them with a aggressive manner.

FLASK
More of a water rat in my opinion. An creature that requires a small application of time and trouble to boil it down to oil. They annoy me. They really do. But I make them pay!

Music. The three mates stand stage center. The three harpooners approach them.

ISHMAEL
Now these three mates...Starbuck, Stubb, and Flask...commanded three of the Pequod's boats as headsman. They stabbed the whales with spears after their harpooners had first flung their weapons.

Clutching his harpoon, Queequeg poses in front of Starbuck.

STARBUCK
Starbuck, the first mate, had selected Queequeg for his squire.

Tashtego hands his mask to Stubb.

STUBB
Stubb's harpooner was Tashtego, a unmixed Indian from Grey Head.

> TASHTEGO
> No longer snuffling in the trail of the wild beasts of the woodland, Tashtego now hunted in the wake of the great whales of the sea. To look at him, you would almost have believed the superstitions of some of the earlier Puritans, and half believed this Indian to be son of the Prince of Powers of the Air.

Stubb helps Tashtego put on his mask. Daggoo hands his mask to Flask.

> FLASK
> Flask's harpooner was Ahasuerus Daggoo...a coal-black negro from Africa who had retained all of his barbaric virtues.

> DAGGOO
> In his youth, Daggoo had voluntarily shipped on board of a whaler, lying in a lonely bay on his native coast. Erect as a giraffe, he moved about the decks with all the pomp of royalty. Any white man standing before him seemed a white flag come to beg truce of a fortress.

Music. Flask helps Daggoo put on his mask. The three harpooners sit down for dinner.

> ISHMAEL
> Pip was cabin steward for these men. He was a tender-hearted boy who loved life, and all life's peaceable securities, so that the panic-striking business in which he had somehow unaccountably become entrapped, had most sadly blurred his brightness. Hard fares the waiter who waits upon cannibals.

Pip begins to serve the men food.

> PIP
> Here you go, sirs. Daggoo, Queequeg, Tashtego...

> TASHTEGO
> Beef and bread. Bread and beef. The bread as hard as granite. The beef as salty as the sea.

                    PIP
          It's what the cook gives me. I
          serve the cook. That's all.

Tashtego glances at the other two harpooners.

                    TASHTEGO
          We need fresh meat. How can we kill
          the whales without fresh meat in
          our bellies?

                    QUEEQUEG
          Ummmmm.

                    DAGGOO
          A young creature. Tender. That's
          what we need.

                    QUEEQUEG
          Ummmm.

                    PIP
          More beef? More bread? Perhaps
          there's some figs in the hold.
          Would you like some figs, sirs?

                    TASHTEGO
          Young is best, Daggoo. The old
          scrap of flesh is bone and gristle.
          That's all.

                    DAGGOO
          How would you cook it, Tashtego?
          Broiled? Boiled or...

                    QUEEQUEG
          Raw.

                    PIP
               (terrified)
          Salt? Pepper? Anyone? How about a
          biscuit? A nice warm biscuit?

Daggoo reaches out and grabs Pip. Tashtego sharpens his
knife.

                    TASHTEGO
          Come here, Pip. Join our dinner.

                    PIP
          I've...eaten...already.

                    DAGGOO
          We haven't.

Stubb blows a tin whistle and the harpooners freeze.

                STUBB
Forenoon watch! All hands up!

Music. The harpooners exit with the benches. Lights up on Ahab facing upstage.

                ISHMAEL
For several days after leaving Nantucket, nothing above hatches was seen of Captain Ahab. Then, one gray and gloomy morning, I answered the call of the watch and saw him standing on the quarter deck.

Ahab turns and looks at Starbuck.

                AHAB
Master Starbuck! Send everyone aft!

                STARBUCK
I beg your pardon, Captain Ahab.

                AHAB
Send everyone aft. Mast-heads, there! Come down!

The crew slides down on ropes. Stubb approaches Ahab.

                STUBB
Excuse me, Captain. But perhaps we could keep one or two men on the spars. Don't want the sails to luft.

                AHAB
That's my order, Mr. Stubb. Follow it.

                STUBB
I realize that, Captain. I'm only suggesting...

                AHAB
Down, dog, and kennel!

                STUBB
I...I am not used to be spoken to that way, sir. I do not but less than half like it.

                AHAB
Away, Mr. Stubb!

STUBB
No, Captain. Not yet. I will not
tamely be called a dog, sir.

AHAB
Then be called ten times a donkey,
and a mule, and an ass, and begone,
or I'll clear the world of thee!

Ahab takes a step towards Stubb and the second mate retreats.

STUBB
Yes, Captain. Whatever you say,
Captain.

Flask grins at Stubb.

FLASK
Oh, you stood up to him quite well.

STUBB
I was muddled in the head, that
all. I didn't know whether to
strike him or...to pray for him.
God knows, I felt like doing both.

Ahab turns and faces the crew.

AHAB
What do you do when you see a
whale, men?

CREW
Sing out for him!

AHAB
Good! And what do you do next, men?

CREW
Lower away, and after him!

AHAB
And what tune is it you pull to,
men?

CREW
A dead whale or a stove boat!

Ahab takes a gold coin out of his pocket.

AHAB
Do you see this Spanish ounce of
gold? It's a sixteen dollar piece.
Do you see it? Mr. Starbuck, hand me
a top-maul!

Ahab steps over to the mast while Starbuck brings him a hammer.

                    AHAB
Whoever of you raises me a white-headed whale with a wrinkled brow and a crooked jaw...he shall have this gold ounce, my boys!

Ahab hammers the gold to the mast as the crew cheers him. He throws down the maul and faces the men.

                    AHAB
It's a white whale, I say. A white whale. Skin your eyes of him, men. Look sharp for the white water. If you see but a bubble, sing out.

                  TASHTEGO
Captain Ahab, that white whale must be the same that some call Moby Dick.

                    AHAB
Moby Dick? Do you know the white whale then, Tash?

                  TASHTEGO
Does he fan-tail a little curious, sir. Before he goes down?

                    DAGGOO
And has he a curious spout, too...very bushy, even for a paracetty, and mighty quick, Captain Ahab?

                  QUEEQUEG
And he have one, two, three...oh, good many iron in him, too, Captain. All twisketee be-twisk, like him...him...

                    AHAB
Corkscrew! Death and devils! Men, it is Moby Dick you have seen! Moby Dick!

                  STARBUCK
Was it not Moby Dick that took off your leg?

                    AHAB
Aye, Starbuck. Aye, my hearties all round. It was Moby Dick that razeed me; made a poor pegging lubber of me for ever and a day!
                        (MORE)

AHAB
And this is what you have shipped for, men. To chase that white whale on both sides of land, and over all sides of earth, till he spouts black blood and rolls fin out. What say you, men, will you splice hands on it, now?

CREW
Aye!

AHAB
God bless you! Pip! Go draw the great measure of grog!

Pip runs off. Ahab turns and examines Starbuck.

AHAB
But what's this long face about, Mr. Starbuck. Wilt thou not chase the white whale?

STARBUCK
I'm game for his crooked jaw, and for the jaws of death, too...if it fairly comes in the way of the business we follow. But I came here to hunt whales, not my commander's vengeance. How many barrels will thy vengeance yield thee, Captain Ahab? It will not fetch you much in our Nantucket market.

AHAB
"The Nantucket Market?" God save us from souls of accountants!
        (motions to Starbuck)
But come closer, Starbuck. I see you require a deeper layer of understanding. Come closer...

Ahab and Starbuck stand together.

AHAB
All visible objects are but as pasteboard masks. But in each event ...in the living act...some unknown but still reasoning thing puts forth the moldings of its features from behind the unreasoning mask. How can the prisoner reach outside except by thrusting through the wall? To me, the white whale is that wall, shoved near to me.

> STARBUCK
> Why seek vengeance on a dumb brute that simply attacked you from the blindest instinct? To be engaged with such a thing seems blasphemous.

> AHAB
> Talk not to me of blasphemy, man! I'd strike the sun if it insulted me. For if the sun do that...
> (watches Starbuck)
> Turn your eyes away, Starbuck! More intolerable than a fiend's glaring is a doltish stare!

> STARBUCK
> Captain, I can not...can not...

> AHAB
> So, you reddenest and palest. My heat has melted thee to anger-glow. But look you, Starbuck...what is said in heat, that thing unsays itself. I meant not to incense thee. Let it go.
> (points to the crew)
> Look at the crew, man! The crew! Are they not one and all with Ahab in this matter of the whale? Will you hang back when every foremast-hand has clutched a whetstone? Speak, but speak! Aye...thy silence, then, that voices thee.

Starbuck turns away.

> STARBUCK
> God keep me. God keep us all.

Pip enters with a tankard of rum. Ahab returns to the crew as Starbuck stands apart.

> AHAB
> The measure! The measure!

He takes the rum from Pip and hands it to the nearest sailor.

> AHAB
> Drink and pass! Round with it, round! Short draughts, long swallows, men. 'Tis hot as Satan's hoof. So, so, it goes round excellently. It spiralizes in you... Forks out at the serpent-snapping eye!

Ahab grabs the empty tankard.

                    AHAB
          Pip! Refill this! Queequeg! Daggoo!
          Tashtego! Cut your seizings and
          draw the poles!

Pip exits. The three men detach the barbs of their harpoons.

                    AHAB
          I do appoint you all gentleman and
          noble cup bearers. Cant the steel.
          Cant them over. Know you not the
          goblet end?

The men turn the harpoons upside down. Pip returns with more grog.

                    AHAB
          Now, advance to me. Hold your irons
          while I fill!

He pours rum in the sockets of the harpoons.

                    AHAB
          Commend the murderous chalices!
          Bestow them, you who are now made
          parties to this indissoluble
          league. Now, drink! Drink and swear!

The men raise the harpoons.

                    AHAB
          God hunt us all, if we do not hunt
          Moby Dick to his death!

                    CREW
          AYE!

The crew cheers. The music becomes louder, then fades. Blackout. Light on Ishmael.

                    ISHMAEL
          I, Ishmael, was one of that crew.
          My oath had been welded with theirs
          and the stronger I shouted, and
          more did I hammer and clinch my
          oath, because of the dread in my
          soul. It was the whiteness of the
          whale that above all things
          appalled me.

Queequeg, Daggoo and Tashtego step from the darkness and stand behind Ishmael.

                        QUEEQUEG
          Witness the white bear of the
          poles, and the white shark of the
          tropics; what but their smooth,
          flaky whiteness makes them the
          transcendent horrors they are?

                        DAGGOO
          Think of the albatross...that white
          phantom that sails in all
          imaginations.

                        TASHTEGO
          The milky sea. The frosts of the
          mountains.

The three harpooners disappear into the darkness. Music.

                        ISHMAEL
          Is it because whiteness is not so
          much a color as the visible absence
          of color, that there is such a dumb
          blankness, full of meaning, in a
          wide landscape of snows...a
          colorless, all-color of death
          from which we shrink?

He hears the sound of laughing. Several sailors and Pip lie in hammocks slung within the ribs of the whale. Other sailors stand around a lantern. Ishmael joins the group.

                        ISHMAEL
          Midnight. And the crew lounged on
          the forecastle, still merry from
          Ahab's rum.

                        CREW
          Farewell and adieu to you, Spanish ladies!
          Farewell and adieu to you, ladies of Spain!
          Our captain's commanded...

A Nantucket sailor jumps up.

                        NANTUCKET SAILOR
          Come on, boys! Don't be sentimental!
          It's bad for the digestion! Take a
          tonic and follow me!

He sings as a sailor plays a tin whistle.

NANTUCKET SAILOR
Our Captain stood upon the deck,
A spy-glass in his hand,
A viewing of those gallant whales
That blew at every strand.
Oh, your tubs in your boats, my boys,
And by your braces stand,
And we'll have one of those fine whales,
Hand, over hand! Boys!
Hand, over hand!

The sailors freeze. Light on Starbuck standing downstage.

STARBUCK
My soul is more than matched. She's overmanned...and by a madman. Insufferable sting, that sanity should ground arms on such a field. But Ahab drilled deep down and blasted all my reason out of me. Horrible old man! I plainly see my miserable office...to obey, rebelling. And worse yet, to hate with touch of pity! Yet is there hope. Time and time flow wide. The hated whale has the round watery world to swim in, as the small gold fish has its glassy globe.

The Nantucket sailor bows and everyone laughs.

STARBUCK
The crew is one with Ahab. The white whale is their demigorgon. Stand by me, hold me, bind me, Oh ye blessed influences!

Blackout on Starbuck.

NANTUCKET SAILOR
Avast the chorus! Eight bells there! D'ye hear? Let me call the watch. I've got the sort of mouth for that...the hogshead mouth.

He runs through the ribs of the whale, pushing the men out of their hammocks.

NANTUCKET SAILOR
Star bo-l-e-e-n-s a-h-o-y! Eight bells there below! Tumble up!

                    ENGLISH SAILOR
          Grand snoozing tonight, matey. Fat
          night for that. We sing. They
          sleep. At 'em again! Tell 'em it's
          the resurrection. They must kiss
          their last, and come to judgment..

Pip and a few other sailors join the group.

                    SPANISH SAILOR
          Hist, boys! Let's have a jig or two
          before we ride to anchor in Blanket
          Bay! Pip! Little Pip! Hurrah with
          your tambourine!

                    PIP
          Don't know where it is...

                    SPANISH SAILOR
          Beat thy belly, then, and wag thy
          ears. Damn me, won't you dance!
          Throw yourself! Legs! Legs!

The Nantucket sailor appears with Pip's tambourine.

                    NANTUCKET SAILOR
          Here comes the music! Now for it!

                    MALTESE SAILOR
          Where's your girls? Who but a fool
          would take his left hand by his
          right, and say to himself, how d'ye
          do? Partners! I must have partners!

An English sailor extends his hand.

                    ENGLISH SAILOR
          Hoe corn when you may, say I. All
          legs go to harvest soon.

Pip pounds his tambourine and some of the sailors begin to dance.

                    NANTUCKET SAILOR
          Go it, Pip! Rig it, dig it, stig
          it, quiq it!

                    ENGLISH SAILOR
          Hold up thy hoop! Till I jump
          through it!

The sailors freeze. Light on Stubb standing in the crow's nest. He sips from a small bottle of rum.

                    STUBB
Ha! Ha! Haaaaaaa! Hem! Clear my
throat. I've been thinking over it
ever since, and that ha, ha's the
final consequence. Why so? Because
a laugh's the wisest, easiest
answer to all that's strange. Come
what will...it's all predestinated.
I know not all that may be coming,
but be it what it will, I'll go to
it laughing. Such a waggish leering
as lurks in all your horribles. A
laugh's the only true thing in this
world. Right now, my woman back at
home is probably gay as a French
flag, giving a party for the last
arrived harpooners. She's smiling...
singing a song...and so shall I.
          (sings)
We drink tonight with hearts as light,
To love, as gay and fleeting
As bubbles that swim, on the beaker's brim,
And break on the lips while meeting...

Lights up on Flask standing in the jaws of the whale.

                    FLASK
Stubb! Mr. Stubb!

                    STUBB
What? Who calls? Is that you, Flask?

                    FLASK
Something's wrong.

                    STUBB
Wrong? Nothing's wrong on a night
like this.

                    FLASK
Down here. Hurry.

                    STARBUCK
All right...just through with his
job. I'm coming.

He climbs down the mast. Lights up on the crew dancing. The music becomes faster and faster, then suddenly stops. The men laugh and fall on the floor. Blackout. Light on Ahab standing at a small writing desk.

AHAB
T'was not so hard a task to bind the crew to my will. I thought I'd find one stubborn, at the least. But my one cogged circle fits into all their various wheels, and they revolve. Starbuck thinks I'm mad, but I am madness maddened...that wild madness that's only calm to comprehend itself. The prophecy was that I should be dismembered and... Aye! I lost this leg. I now prophesy that I will dismember my dismemberer. Now, then be the prophet and the fulfiller one. The path to my fixed purpose is laid with iron rails, whereon my soul is grooved to run.

Blackout on Ahab. Light on Flask as he kneels within the jaws of the whale. Stubb approaches him.

STUBB
So, what's wrong? Why'd you bring me down from the main mast?

Fedallah lies unseen on the top of the skull. He coughs softly.

FLASK
Hist! Did you hear that noise!

STUBB
What noise d'ye mean?

Fedallah coughs again.

FLASK
There it is again. Did you hear it? A cough. It sounded like a cough.

STUBB
Cough be damned! It's just the wind.

FLASK
Say what you will, Stubb. I've sharp ears.

STUBB
Aye, you're the chap that heard the hum of the old Quakeress's knitting needles fifty miles at sea from Nantucket.

                    FLASK
          Grin away. We'll see what turns up.
          There's somebody on this ship that
          has not yet been seen on deck and I
          suspect Ahab knows about it.

                    STUBB
          Flask...My friend...Dear King-Post...
                    (pulls out the bottle)
          Have a drink.

                    FLASK
          But I heard...

                    STARBUCK
          A <u>drink</u>, Mr. Flask. It warms the
          stomach and calms the heart and
          answers any sound in the night.

Blackout on the two men. Lights up on the crew. The Maltese
sailor stares at the ocean.

                    MALTESE SAILOR
          Stand by for reefing, hearties! The
          winds are just crossing swords,
          pell-mell they'll go lunging
          presently.

                    NANTUCKET SAILOR
          What of it? Not a man here is
          afraid. We're just the lads to hunt
          the Captain up his white whale.

                    MALTESE SAILOR
          Lightning off the port bow! Do you
          see it! Look yonder, boys, there's
          another in the sky...lurid like, ye
          see, all else pitch black.

                    DAGGOO
          What of it? Who's afraid of black's
          afraid of me! I'm quarried out of it!

                    SPANISH SAILOR
          Aye, harpooner, thy race is the
          undeniable dark side of mankind...
          devilish dark at that. No offense.

                    DAGGOO
                    (grimly)
          None.

The English sailor tries to pull the Spaniard away from Daggoo.

                    ENGLISH SAILOR
          Calm yourself, man. Are you mad
          or drunk?

                    MALTESE SAILOR
               (still watching the horizon)
          What's that I saw? More lightning?
          Yes.

                    SPANISH SAILOR
          No. It's Daggoo showing his teeth.

Daggoo springs towards the Spanish sailor.

                    DAGGOO
          Swallow thine, manikin! White
          skin, white liver!

The Spaniard pulls out a knife.

                    SPANISH SAILOR
          Knife thee heartily, big frame,
          small spirit!

The crew shouts. The two men circle each other and swing
their knives. Stubb appears and the men stop fighting.

                    STUBB
          Sheath those knives and grab the
          lines! Hands by the halyards! In
          top-gallant sails! Stand by to reef
          the topsails! The squall! The
          squall! Jump my jollies!

Blackout. Light on Pip holding his tambourine.

                    PIP
          Jollies? Lord help such jollies!
          Crish, crash! There goes the jib-
          stay! Blang-whang! God! Duck lower,
          Pip, here comes the royal yard!
          It's worse than being the whirled
          woods, the last day of the year.
          It's a white squall...that's what
          they call it. White squall. White
          whale. The thought of it makes me
          jingle all over like my tambourine.

Blackout on Pip. Then lights up on the entire stage. Tashtego
clings to a rope.

                    TASHTEGO
          There she blows! There! There!

The crew place four benches on the stage. Ahab hurries forward.

                    AHAB
          Where-away?

                    TASHTEGO
          On the lee-beam, about two miles
          off! A school of them! There go the
          flukes!

                    AHAB
                    (to Pip)
          Quick, Steward! Time! Time!

Pip checks a pocket watch as Ahab motions to the crew.

                    AHAB
          To your boats!

                    QUEEQUEG
          The sailors at fore and missen came
          down.

                    DAGGOO
          The cranes were thrust out. The
          main-yard was backed.

                    TASHTEGO
          The three boats swung over the sea
          like three samphire baskets over
          high cliffs.

                    ISHMAEL
          Suddenly Ahab was surrounded by
          dusky phantoms that seemed fresh
          formed out of air. Jumping into the
          Captain's boat that hung from the
          starboard quarter, they cast loose
          the tackles and bands.

Fedallah and a Manilla sailor appear. They stand together
with Ahab.

                    AHAB
          All ready there, Fedallah?

Fedallah nods his head.

                    AHAB
          Good. Then lower away!

The benches are used as whale boats. The four whaling groups
are: (1) Ahab, Fedallah and the Manilla sailor; (2) Starbuck,
Queequeg and Ishmael; (3) Stubb, Tashtego and Pip; (4) Flask,
Daggoo, and a sailor.

ISHMAEL
The sheaves whirled round in the blocks and the four boats dropped in the sea. All eyes were on Ahab and the strangers in his crew.

STARBUCK
Captain Ahab?

AHAB
Spread yourself! Give way, all four boats! Thou, Flask, pull out to leeward!

FLASK
Aye, aye, sir!
    (to crew)
Lay back! There! There she blows right ahead, boys! Lay back!

FLASK
What did I tell you, Mr. Stubb. Didn't I tell you that there was something in the hold? Knitting needles indeed!

STUBB
It's a surprise, I'll grant you. But the real marvel is that Ahab's in his own boat. If I had but one leg you wouldn't catch me in a boat unless to stop the plug-hole with my timber toe.

FLASK
He has one knee and a good part of the other left, you know.

STUBB
Really? I never saw him kneel.
    (to crew)
Pull, pull my fine hearts-alive. What is it you stare at? Those chaps in the captain's boat? Tut! They're only five more hands come to help us. Never mind from where. Devils are good fellows enough. Pull!
    (to Starbuck)
Mr. Starbuck! Larboard boat there! A word with you, sir, if you please! What do you think of those yellow boys, sir?

STARBUCK
Smuggled on board, somehow, before
the ship sailed.
        (whispers to crew)
Strong, strong boys.
        (to Stubb)
But never mind, Mr. Stubb, all for
the best.
        (to crew)
Spring, my men, spring.
        (to Stubb)
There's whales ahead, Mr. Stubb,
and that's what you came for.
        (to crew)
Pull, my boys.
        (to Stubb)
This is our duty. Duty and profit
hand in hand.

TASHTEGO
        (pointing)
Down, down all, and give way! There
they are!

QUEEQUEG
They saw a troubled bit of greenish
white water, and thin scattered
puffs of vapor hovering over it...

DAGGOO
The air vibrated and tingled like
the air over intensely heated
plates of iron.

TASHTEGO
Beneath this atmospheric waving and
curling, and partially beneath a
thin layer of water, the whales
were swimming.

The Manila sailor and the sailor on Flask's boat move
downstage and clasp the ends of a long strip of black fabric.

STARBUCK
        (whispers)
Pull, pull, my good boys.

FLASK
Roar and pull, my thunderbolts!
Beach me on their backs!

STUBB
Pull, babes. Pull, all. Crack your
backbones and bite your knives in two!

The two sailors raise the black fabric and it billows up into the air.

>   ISHMAEL
>   And lo! Close to Stubb's boat, not
>   forty fathoms off, a gigantic Sperm
>   Whale lay rolling in the water like
>   the capsized hull of a frigate, his
>   broad, glossy back, of an Ethiopian
>   hue, glistening in the sun's rays
>   like a mirror.

>   STUBB
>   Start her, start her, my men! Give
>   'em the long and strong stroke of
>   the oar. But keep cool, keep cool
>   ...cucumbers is the word...easy,
>   easy...Now, stand up, Tashtego!
>   Give it to him!

Tashtego stands, throws the harpoon, and screams.

>   QUEEQUEG
>   The oarsmen pull their oars back,
>   as the line hisses along every one
>   of their wrists.

>   STUBB
>   Wet the line! Wet the line!

>   DAGGOO
>   The rope snaps tight and the boat
>   flies through the boiling water
>   like a shark all fins.

>   STUBB
>   Haul in! Haul in!

The two sailors reverse the fabric, showing a blood-red underside.

>   STUBB
>   Now, pull up! Pull up! We got the
>   bastard!

The sailors wrap the red fabric around Stubb's boat. Stubb jabs with a lance.

>   QUEEQUEG
>   Reaching over the bow, Stubb jabbed
>   his long sharp lance into the fish,
>   and kept it there, churning and
>   churning, seeking the innermost
>   life of the fish.

DAGGOO
The whale rolled out into view, surging
from side to side, until clotted red
gore shot into the frightened air.

FLASK
He's dead, Mr. Stubb...

Stubb takes out his pipe and stares at the blood-red water.

STUBB
Yes. Both pipes smoked out.

TASHTEGO
And withdrawing his own pipe from
his mouth, Stubb scattered the dead
ashes over the water and, for a
moment, stood thoughtfully eyeing
the vast corpse he had made.

STARBUCK
Attach the lines!

Ahab exits. Fedallah and the Manilla sailor pull the black fabric to the base of the mast. The rest of the crew appear with equipment and get ready to process the whale.

DAGGOO
The whale was moored alongside the
ship...tied by the head to the
stern and by the tail to the bows.
Seen through the darkness of night,
ship and whale seemed yoked together
like colossal oxen...one standing
while the other reclined.

Stubb grabs Ishmael and ties a rope around his waist. The rope passes through a pulley and is attached to Queequeg.

TASHTEGO
A hole was cut just above the
nearest of the whale's side fins,
then Queequeg descended on the
monster's back to insert a large
hook in the flesh.

Stubb motions for Ishmael to pull the rope. Ishmael pulls and Queequeg is lifted into the air above the black fabric.

ISHMAEL
He floundered about...half on the
whale and half on the water...while
I was attached to him by what was
known as a monkey rope. For better
or worse, we were wedded.

Queequeg pulls on the rope and Ishmael is yanked forward. The two men seesaw back and forth.

>   STUBB
> Pull, Ishmael! Pull hard! There's a
> shark nibbling at his toes.

>   ISHMAEL
> Pulling him now and then between
> the whale and the ship, I saw that
> this situation of mine was the
> precise situation of every mortal
> that breathes. We are all connected
> to each other. If your banker goes
> bankrupt, you break as well. If
> your apothecary, by mistake,
> puts poison in your pills...you die.

>   STARBUCK
> The hook's fastened! Pull him up!

Queequeg is pulled upwards, then lowered to the deck. The crew unfastens his rope.

>   STUBB
> His lips are turning blue. Where's
> Pip? Move lively! Bring him a drink!

Stubb stops Pip as he hurries over to Queequeg. He pulls a cup from the boy's hands.

>   STUBB
> And what's this? Doesn't look like
> rum to me.

He sips from the cup and spits out the liquid.

>   STUBB
> Ginger water! You're giving him
> ginger water! Is this the sort of
> fuel you use to kindle a fire in
> a shivering cannibal?

>   PIP
> Mr. Stubb...Sir...Captain Bildad
> told me that no spirits would be
> served to the harpooners.

>   STUBB
> No spirits? How can you kick a
> shark in the nose without spirits?
> There's some sneaking Temperance
> Society movement about this
> business, Mr. Starbuck!

                    STARBUCK
          It is poor stuff to give a man.

                    STUBB
          Do you want to poison us, Pip?
          Murder us all and pocket the
          insurance on our lives?

                    PIP
          Captain Bildad said to give the
          harpooners ginger-jub.

                    STUBB
          Ginger-jub? I'll give you ginger-
          jub, you gingerly rascal! Run to
          the lockers and get some grog! Now!

Pip runs off. Queequeg moves downstage. The black fabric is attached to the hook and raised into the air.

                    TASHTEGO
          Now a hook was inserted, the crew
          pulled on the line...and the
          whale's blubber was stripped from
          its body precisely as an orange
          rind is peeled off with a spiral cut.

Flask approaches the fabric with a long knife and "cuts" a hole in the middle of the cloth.

                    DAGGOO
          A second hook was fastened onto the
          blubber, then the strip was severed
          completely in twain.

The crew attaches a second hook and pulley to the bottom part of the fabric. The cloth is divided in half, and the top portion is dragged over to a table by two sailors.

                    QUEEQUEG
          The upper strip was pulled clear
          and dragged over to the mincers
          while the new hook continued its
          job of stripping the whale.

Ishmael approaches the table and watches the mincers cutting the blubber into strips.

                    ISHMAEL
          This cozy blanketing of the whale's
          body was now thrown into a try-pot
          where it was reduced to oil.

The mincers toss strips of the fabric into a large pot. A man dips in ladle into the pot, then pours the oil into a wooden tub.

ISHMAEL
No wood was necessary...for scraps
of the whale's own flesh provided
the fuel. The oil was stirred and
poured into cooling tubs...

Ishmael and Queequeg squat beside a wooden tub.

ISHMAEL
Where it crystallized into lumps
rolling about in the liquid part.
It was our business to squeeze
these lumps back into fluid. Ahhh,
what a sweet and unctuous duty.

Ishmael and Queequeg squeeze the lumps until they touch hands.

ISHMAEL
Squeeze! Squeeze! I squeezed that
oil until a strange sort of insanity
came over me and I found myself
unwittingly squeezing my co-laborer's
hands, as much to say..."Come, let
us squeeze ourselves into the very
milk of human kindness."

The lights fade. The crew removes all of the equipment. Pip
appears and gives a lantern to Starbuck.

STARBUCK
The whale had become oil. The
oil...light. For the whaler hunts
for his light just as the traveler
on the prairie hunts up his own
supper of game.

Music. Lights up on Ahab writing in his cabin. Fedallah
stands beside him. Starbuck enters carrying the lantern.

AHAB
Who's there? On deck! Begone!

STARBUCK
Captain Ahab mistakes. It is I.

Ahab nods and Fedallah disappears into the shadows.

AHAB
Well? What matter concerns you?

STARBUCK
The oil in the hold is leaking, Sir.
We must up Burtons and break out
the casks.

AHAB
Break out the casks? Nonsense. Are we to heave-to here for a week to tinker with a parcel of old hoops?

STARBUCK
Either do that, Sir, or waste in one day more oil than we may make good in a year. What we come 20,000 miles to get is worth saving, Sir.

AHAB
So it is; if we get it.

STARBUCK
I was speaking of the oil in the hold, Sir.

AHAB
And I was not speaking or thinking of that at all. Begone! Let it leak! I'm all aleak myself.

STARBUCK
What will the owners say, Sir?

AHAB
Let the owners stand on Nantucket beach and outyell the Typhoons. Owners, owners? Thou are always prating to me, Starbuck, about those miserly owners, as if the owners were my conscience. On deck!

STARBUCK
No, Sir. Not yet. I do entreat. And I do dare, Sir...to be forbearing. Shall we not understand each other better, Captain Ahab?

Ahab picks up a musket and points it at Starbuck.

AHAB
There is one God that is Lord over the earth, and one Captain that is Lord over the Pequod. On deck!

Starbuck hesitates, then turns away. He stops and faces Ahab.

STARBUCK
I won't ask thee to beware of Starbuck, thou would laugh. But let Ahab beware of Ahab. Beware of thyself, old man.

He starts to leave. Ahab lowers the musket.

> **AHAB**
> Mr. Starbuck! Wait...
> (approaches him)
> Thou art but too good a fellow, Starbuck. Too...good...
> (turns away)
> Up Burtons and break out the main-hold. Bring the casks on deck.

Blackout on Ahab and Starbuck. Lights up on the ship. A barrel is attached to the mast's rope and tackle. The crew pulls it higher while Ishmael watches from the crow's nest.

> **DAGGOO**
> Upon searching, it was found that the casks last struck into the hold were perfectly sound, and that the leak must be further off.

> **QUEEQUEG**
> So, it being calm weather, they broke out deeper and deeper...

> **TASHTEGO**
> So deep that you almost looked next for some moldy corner-stone cask containing coin of Captain Noah, with copies of the posted placards, vainly warning about the flood.

Ishmael sees something and points downstage.

> **ISHMAEL**
> Ship off the starboard bow!

The three mates look out at the approaching ship.

> **STUBB**
> A ship? I smell it, but I don't see it.

> **STARBUCK**
> Over there...on the starboard bow.

> **FLASK**
> It's a French ship. See the colors on its peak.

> **STUBB**
> That flag's not making her stink.

> **FLASK**
> She's coming around...

                    STARBUCK
          There! That's the problem! She's
          got a blasted whale alongside her.
          The creature must have died on its
          own a more than a month ago and now
          they're trying to butcher dead meat.

Standing on the skull, Stubb gazes out at the ship.

                    STUBB
          God save us! I well know that these
          Frenchmen are but poor devils in
          the fishery, but look at that! Why,
          I'd get more oil by chopping up
          these three masts of ours, than
          he'll get from that bundle of bones.

He slides down a rope and motions to his crew.

                    STUBB
          Though, now that I think of it, it
          may contain something worth a good
          deal more more valuable than oil.
          It's worth trying.
                    (to the crew)
          Lower my boat! Let's take a look at
          these fools!

Stubb, Tashtego, and Pip move to the edge of the stage. The
first mate of the ship --- a "Gurnseyman" --- climbs onto the
platform that designates another ship. The Gurnseyman has a
bandanna tied in front of his nose.

                    STUBB
          What's the name, Pip? Can you read
          it on the head board?

                    PIP
          Bouton de Rose.

                    STUBB
          "Bouton de Rose." I think that's
          Frenchy talk for "Rosebud." Sweet
          name for a smelly ship.

Ahab appears on the stage as Stubb walks up the aisle.

                    AHAB
          Mr. Stubb! Inquire about the whale!

                    STUBB
          Yes, Captain!

With one hand covering his nose, Stubb reaches the platform.

                    STUBB
          Bouton de Rose, ahoy! Do any of you
          speak English?

                    GURNSEYMAN
          I do.

                    STUBB
          Well, then, my Bouton-de-Rose bud,
          have you seen Moby Dick! The White Whale!

                    GURNSEYMAN
          Never heard of such a whale. No.

                    STUBB
               (to Ahab)
          No, Sir! They haven't!

Ahab returns to his cabin. Stubb smiles at the Gurnseyman.

                    STUBB
          What's the matter with your nose, here?

                    GURNSEYMAN
          I wish it was broken or that I
          didn't have any nose at all. What
          are you holding yours for?

                    STUBB
          Oh, nothing. Fine day, ain't it?
          Throw us a bunch of poises, will
          you, Bouton-de-Rose?

                    GURNSEYMAN
          What in the devil's name do you
          want here!

                    STUBB
          Keep cool. That's the word. In
          fact, why don't you pack that whale
          in ice...there's no oil in him.

                    GURNSEYMAN
          I know that well enough, but the
          captain won't believe it. He was a
          manufacturer from Cologne before he
          bought this ship.

                    STUBB
          Perhaps he'll believe me. Call him
          up and let me come aboard.

Stubb climbs up on the platform as the Gurnseyman calls out
to his Captain.

GURNSEYMAN
Captain! Monsieur! Excusez-moi!

The Captain of the Rosebud hurries down the aisle clutching a handkerchief over his nose.

STUBB
Does he speak English?

GURNSEYMAN
Not a word.

STUBB
Tell him that the crew might catch
a fever from this blasted whale.
Who knows? He might believe me.

The Captain climbs up onto the platform and looks at Stubb.

GURNSEYMAN
Captain, je vous presente Monsieur...

STUBB
Stubb.

GURNSEYMAN
Monsieur Stubb. Une baleiner Americain.

FRENCH CAPTAIN
Enchante.

STUBB
You may as well begin by telling
him that he looks a sort of babyish
to me.

GURNSEYMAN
Une baleine...C'est infecte. C'est
tres dangereux pour les baleiners.

STUBB (simultaneous)
And now that I've eyed him
carefully, I'm quite certain that
he's no more fit to command a whale
ship than a St. Jago monkey.

FRENCH CAPTAIN
Je comprends. Demenage la baleine...
vite!

GURNSEYMAN
Cast off that blasted whale! Move
lively!

FRENCH CAPTAIN
Merci beaucoup, Monsieur Stubb.
Desirez-vous une verre de Bordeaux?

GURNSEYMAN
You want a glass of Frenchy wine?

STUBB
Thank him heartily, but tell him
it's against my principles to drink
with the man I've diddled.
    (climbs off platform)
In fact, tell him I must go.

Stubb climbs off the platform and begins to search through the audience. The Gurnseyman and the French Captain exit.

DAGGOO
Getting into his boat, Stubb pulled
the whale away from Frenchman's ship.
Seizing a sharp boat-spade, he
commenced an excavation into the
body, a little behind the side fin.

ISHMAEL
There she blows! On the starboard-
beam! About three miles away!

TASHTEGO
Numberless fowls were diving, and
ducking, and screaming, as he
thrust his hand deep inside.

AHAB
Stand by the boats! Where's Stubb?

STARBUCK
Mr. Stubb!

STUBB
Just one minute! There! I have it!

Grabbing a woman's purse, Stubb returns to the stage.

QUEEQUEG
It was a purse of ambergris...that
soft, waxy substance found in the
bowels of a sick whale and used in
perfumery and precious candles.

STUBB
It's worth a gold guinea an ounce
to any druggist. Glory plucked from
the heart of decay!

The lights begin to fade as Stubb, Tashtego and Pip stand together. Queequeg and Daggoo approach them.

            DAGGOO
    All boats touched the water and
    converged upon a school of whales.

            STUBB
    Pull hard, boys! Burst your lungs
    and livers! Tashtego! Throw your
    lance...now!

Tashtego throws a harpoon.

            QUEEQUEG
    Stubb's boat reached the group
    first and when one of the fish
    received the darted iron, it gave
    its customary rap under poor Pip's
    seat.

Startled, Pip stands up.

            STUBB
    Stick to the boat, Pip, or by the
    Lord, I won't pick you up! We can't
    afford to lose whales by the likes
    of you!

            DAGGOO
    Then the stricken whale started on
    a fierce run, the line snapped past
    the boy and...

Queequeg and Daggoo lift up Pip by his arms and place him on the stage.

            QUEEQUEG
    He jumped. He jumped.

            STUBB
    Let him go! Another boat will pick
    him up!

Blackout on Stubb and Tashtego. Light on Pip as he huddles on the stage.

            PIP
    Mr. Stubb! Please...

Queequeg and Daggoo surround Pip with a white fabric.

DAGGOO
And so it happened, that the other
boats, without seeing Pip, suddenly
spied whales close to them on one
side and turned and gave chase.

QUEEQUEG
And Pip was left alone in the
middle of the heartless immensity
of ocean until...by the merest
chance...the ship itself rescued him.

DAGGOO
The sea kept his finite body up,
but drowned the infinite of his
soul. Pip saw God's foot on the
treadle of the loom, and spoke to
it. And therefore his shipmates
called him mad.

They pull the fabric away and disappear into the darkness.
Clutching his tambourine, Pip crouches on the deck. He
watches Starbuck walk towards the captain's cabin.

PIP
Hello, sir. Kind sir...

STARBUCK
What is it?

PIP
Will you do one little errand for
me? Seek out one Pip, who's been
missing long.

STARBUCK
What was done to you was not right,
but it was not malicious. Mr. Stubb
meant you no harm.

PIP
If you find Pip, then comfort him,
for he must be very sad.

STARBUCK
I have tried to be fair and...and
responsible. What more can a man do?

Pip picks up his tambourine.

PIP
For look! He's left his tambourine
behind! I found it! I found it!

STARBUCK
I can't heal you, lad. I'm sorry.

Lights up on Ahab asleep on a chair within his cabin. Starbuck approaches the cabin and Pip follows him.

STARBUCK
Don't follow me. Go away.
(gestures)
Go away!

We hear the sound of a wooden flute as Starbuck enters the cabin. He stops and sees the musket.

STARBUCK
There's the musket he pointed at me...the one with the studded stock.

Starbuck hesitates, then picks up the musket.

STARBUCK
Loaded. Aye. and there's powder in the pan. Best spill it. Wait. I'll cure myself of this and hold the weapon firmly while I think. I come to report a fair wind to him. But how fair? Fair for death and doom... that's fair for Moby Dick.
(examines the gun)
He would have killed me with this. Aye, and would kill all his crew. But what if this instant he was put aside?

He approaches Ahab.

STARBUCK
I can't withstand the old man. Flat obedience to his own flat commands, this is all he desires. There's no other way. Only a fool would try to make him a prisoner. Say he were knotted all over with ropes; chained down to the ring-bolts on this cabin floor...he would be more hideous than a caged tiger. What, then remains? The land is hundreds of leagues away...with two oceans and a whole continent between me and law. Is heaven a murderer when its lightning strikes a would-be murderer in his bed? And would I be a murderer, then, if...

Starbuck points the musket at Ahab and we hear the sound of a bull-roarer (a flat piece of wood at the end of a string which makes a roaring sound).

As lights rise we see Tashtego standing on the whale's backbone --- whirling the bull-roarer like a shaman calling the spirits.

The sound becomes louder and louder, then Starbuck lowers the gun and exits. Silence. Light on Ahab as he opens his eyes.

              AHAB
Stern all! Stern all! The White
Whale spouts blood!

Blackout.

ACT II

Darkness, then we hear the crew whispering:

> **CREW**
> How can the whale survive?
> How can the whale survive?

Lights up as the crew slowly appear on stage. They continue whispering as Ishmael walks the length of the skeleton.

> **ISHMAEL**
> Once, on an island in the South Seas, I visited a temple constructed out of the skeleton of a great Sperm Whale. It was a wondrous sight... sheltered in a glen of lordly palms, The ribs were hung with trophies. The vertebrae were carved with strange hieroglyphics. And, in the skull, the priests kept up an unextinguished aromatic flame, so that the mystic head again sent forth its vapory spout.

He moves in and out of the whale's skeleton. The crew gathers into the four groups that man the different whale boats.

> **ISHMAEL**
> To and fro I paced before this skeleton...brushed the vines aside ...broke through the ribs...and, with a ball of twine wandered amid its many shaded colonnades and arbors. But soon my line was out. And following it back, I emerged from the opening where I entered. I saw no living thing within. Nothing but bones.

He stands outside the skeleton. The whispering stops.

ISHMAEL
Will these bones be our final vision of the whale? Can he survive so wide a chase, so remorseless a havoc, or will he be exterminated from the waters?

Lights shine on the whale boats. The men are shouting --- caught up in a frenzy of killing.

STARBUCK
Spring, men! Pull as hard as you can! Jump clear of the line!

FLASK
Close! On the stern-side! Throw it, Daggoo! Catch him now!

STUBB
The lance! Give the lance! Kill the bastard! Now!

The men freeze for a moment, then lights up. The benches are removed and the men scatter to work at different jobs.

Ahab examines charts in his cabin while Fedallah sits on the whale's skull. Ishmael helps Queequeg carve a wooden box shaped like a coffin. Stubb approaches them and smiles.

STUBB
So, how's our invalid?

ISHMAEL
You mean Queequeg? As you can see, he's in perfect health.

STUBB
Now that's a marvel! Last night, he was sweating and shivering in his hammock. There was nothing much left of him but his tattooing.

QUEEQUEG
I die...later.

STUBB
We'll all die later, but you looked like you were going to die last night.

ISHMAEL
Queequeg remembered that he had something to do ashore...a little duty...so he changed his mind about dying.

> STUBB
> Is that so? Well, I've heard that savages can fix the time of their own passing. But look here, Queequeg. It's a bit ungrateful of you not to die when you said you would. Starbuck prayed for your heathen soul...I heard him...and the carpenter built you that coffin.

Queequeg touches his body.

> QUEEQUEG
> Me.

He touches the coffin.

> QUEEQUEG
> Me.

Stubb examines the coffin.

> STUBB
> Yes, I see it. You're carving your own tattoos into the wood.

> ISHMAEL
> Some prophet on Queequeg's island marked his flesh. It's supposed to be a complete theory of the heavens and earth.

> STUBB
> Well, I can't understand any of it! I am Stubb and Stubb has his history. But here Stubb takes oaths that he has always been jolly.
> (looks around)
> Watch this...I'll get Flask to lie down in the coffin.

> STUBB
> Mr. Flask! A word with you!

> FLASK
> What is it?

Flask approaches the group.

> STUBB
> Mr. Queequeg here has recovered his health. And he's been so kind to convert this box into a little bed for you.

FLASK
A bed? I don't need a bed. I've got my hammock.

STUBB
Look how cozy it is. As warm and snug as a rabbit's cove.

FLASK
It's a coffin.

STUBB
That makes it even better. Most men worry about their final resting place. You'll have yours at hand.

FLASK
Now listen here, Stubb. I'm the third mate and you're over me...

STUBB
And Starbuck's over me. And Ahab's over Starbuck. And God is over... No. I doubt our captain sees anything as being over him.

Fedallah slides down a rope and crosses the deck. Stubb watches him.

STUBB
Except that man...if you could call him one. Some of the crew have been whisperin' that Fedallah is the devil in disguise.

FLASK
If he's the devil, then where's his tail? Folded up in his pocket?

STUBB
He doesn't have a hammock. Sleeps in the rigging at night. Maybe he coils his tail up in the rope so we can't see it.

FLASK
You think so?

STUBB
He's after the Captain to swap way his silver watch...or maybe his soul...and then he'll surrender ...the white whale.

FLASK
(a little frightened)
I don't believe it. I don't. That's
enough of your jokes, Stubb. I've
had my ration for the day.

STUBB
I'm helping you, Flask. I'm thinking
of your comfort. Lie down in your
new...bed. It's a perfect fit.

Flask walks over to the coffin and hesitates.

FLASK
That's for a dead man.

STUBB
If you die in your sleep, you'll be
prepared.

Flash places one foot into the coffin.

STARBUCK
Ship approaching!

STUBB
(to Ishmael)
Close. Very close. Almost caught
him.

FLASK
Caught who? Now listen here, Stubb.
I told you not to...

The Captain of the Samuel Enderby and the ship's surgeon,
Dr. Bunger, stand on the platform that designates another
ship. Ahab walks on deck.

AHAB
What is it, Starbuck? What do you
see?

STARBUCK
Ship on the stern, captain. She's
flying English colors.

AHAB
Ahoy there! Hast thou seen the
White Whale?

Captain Boomer withdraws his hand from the sleeve of his
surcoat: it's a whale bone carved into the shape of a mallet.

CAPTAIN BOOMER
Aye, we've met the creature.

>   AHAB
> Man my boat. Stand to lower.

Fedallah and the Manila sailor carry Ahab to the other ship.

>   ISHMAEL
> In less than a minute, he and his
> crew were dropped to the water, and
> were soon alongside the stranger.

>   CAPTAIN BOOMER
> Bunger! Do the man a favor and
> swing over the cutting tackle!

Dr. Bunger lowers a hook attached to a rope and pulley. Ahab slides his good leg in the curve of the hook and is hoisted up.

>   CAPTAIN BOOMER
> All right, now pull it up! That's
> right! Welcome, Captain! Welcome to
> the Samuel Enderby!

>   AHAB
> Aye! Let us shake bones together!
> An arm that never can shrink and a
> leg that never can run. Where
> did you see the White Whale? How
> long ago?

>   CAPTAIN BOOMER
> I saw him east of here...on the
> Line...last season.

>   AHAB
> And he took that arm off, did he?

>   CAPTAIN BOOMER
> Aye, he was the cause of it. And
> your leg, too?

>   AHAB
> How was it? Tell me...

>   CAPTAIN BOOMER
> One day we lowered for a pod of
> whales, and my boat was fastened to
> one of them. A regular circus horse
> he was, too...That went milling and
> milling around until up from the
> bottom of the sea comes a bouncing
> great whale, with a milky-white
> head and hump, all covered with
> crows' feet and wrinkles.

                    AHAB
That's him!

                    CAPTAIN BOOMER
And harpoons sticking in near his
starboard fin.

                    AHAB
Aye! They were mine! My irons! Go
on...

                    CAPTAIN BOOMER
Give me a chance, then...
          (smiles)
Well, this old great-grandfather,
with the white head and hump, runs
all afoam into the pod, and goes to
snapping furiously at my line.

                    AHAB
He wanted to part it. Free the fast
fish. An old trick.

                    CAPTAIN BOOMER
But in biting the line, it got foul
of his teeth...caught it somehow...
so that when we afterwards pulled
on the line, bounce we came plump
on to his hump! Seeing how matters
stood...and what a noble great
whale it was...I jumped into my
first mate's boat, snatched up the
first harpoon, and let this old
great-grandfather have it. But
Lord, look you sir...the next
instant, in a jiff, I was blind as
a bat...both eyes out...all
befogged and bedeadened with black
foam...the whale's tail looming
straight up out of it, like a
marble steeple...then down it
comes...cutting my boat in two. We
all struck out. To escape his
terrible flailings, I seized hold
of my harpoon pole sticking in him,
and for a moment clung to that like
a sucking fish. But the sea dashed
me off and the whale went down like
a flash and the barb of a harpoon
caught me here...

He touches below the shoulder.

CAPTAIN BOOMER
Just here...and bore me down to
Hell's flames...when...when...all
of a sudden, thank the good God,
the barb ript its along the whole
length of my arm and up I floated
and this gentleman here...

Captain Boomer gestures to the ship's surgeon.

CAPTAIN BOOMER
By the way, Captain...Dr. Bunger,
ship's surgeon: Bunger, my lad...
the Captain...Bunger's going to
tell you the rest.

DR. BUNGER
I ahhh...think that ahhh...

CAPTAIN BOOMER
Go ahead, Bunger boy, spin your
part of the yarn!

DR. BUNGER
I was a shocking bad wound and,
taking my advice, Captain Boomer
here, stood our old Sammy...

CAPTAIN BOOMER
Sammy! He calls the ship "Sammy."
Isn't that the damnest thing you
every heard?

DR. BUNGER
Stood our ship off to the northward,
to get out of the blazing hot
weather...

CAPTAIN BOOMER
Suppose he'd call Queen Victoria,
"Vicky" or something like that.

DR. BUNGER
But it was no use. I did all I
could. Sat up with him nights.
Was very severe with his diet...

CAPTAIN BOOMER
Oh, very severe! Drinking hot rum
toddies till he couldn't see to put
on the bandages!
    (slaps Bunger's back)
Bunger, you dog, laugh! Why don't
ye? You know you're a jolly rascal.

> DR. BUNGER
> (to Ahab)
> I must tell you, Captain...en passant, as the French remark...that I myself...that is to say, Jack Bunger, late of the reverend clergy...am a strict total abstinence man. I never drink...

> CAPTAIN BOOMER
> Water! He never drinks water! It makes him throw a fit! Go on, Bunger. Go on with the arm story.

> DR. BUNGER
> I was about observing, sir, before Captain Boomer's facetious interruption, that spite of my best and severest endeavors, the arm grew black and I cut it off. But I had no hand in shipping that ivory arm there. Captain Boomer's always trying to knock someone's brains out with it. Look. Look at this dent.

Bunger removes his hat and touches his head.

> DR. BUNGER
> The captain knows how that came here.

> CAPTAIN BOOMER
> No, I don't! He was born with it! Oh, you solemn rogue! Bunger, when you die, you ought to die in a pickle, preserved for future ages, you...

> AHAB
> What became of the White Whale?

> CAPTAIN BOOMER
> The whale? Oh...yes...the whale. Well, after he sounded, we didn't see him again for some time.

> AHAB
> Did'st thou cross his wake again?

> CAPTAIN BOOMER
> Twice.

> AHAB
> But could not fasten?

CAPTAIN BOOMER
Didn't want to try. Isn't it
enough to lose one arm?

DR. BUNGER
Do you know, gentlemen...that the
digestive organs of the whale are
so inscrutably constructed by
Divine Providence, that it's quite
impossible for him to completely
digest even a man's arm? And he
knows it too. So what you take for
the White Whale's malice is only
his...his awkwardness.

CAPTAIN BOOMER
Good god, Bunger! You make him
sound like a blushing schoolboy.
Well...whatever...no more white
whales for me. He's best left
alone. Don't you think so, Captain?

AHAB
He is best left alone, but he will
still be hunted, for all that. How
long since thou saw'st him last?
Which way is he heading?

DR. BUNGER
(forcing a smile)
Bless my soul and bring the
thermometer! This man's blood is at
the boiling point!

AHAB
Avast! Tell me, which way was he
heading?

CAPTAIN BOOMER
East. He was heading east, I think...

AHAB
Let me down from here! Man the
boat!

Ahab is lowered down to the two sailors and they carry him back to the ship.

CAPTAIN BOOMER
Captain, stay awhile and reconsider!
It isn't wise...It isn't...Captain!

Blackout on the Englishmen. Music. Spotlight on Ahab as he reaches the stage and falls to his knees in pain. Fedallah approaches Ahab and helps him get up.

ISHMAEL
As Captain Ahab was leaving the
English ship, he landed with such
energy on his boat that his ivory
leg received a half-splintering
shock.

Spotlight on the Nantucket sailor talking to the crew.

NANTUCKET SAILOR
I heard this same thing happened
right before we departed. Some say
the captain was found at dawn in
the middle of the street...his ivory
leg so pushed around that it pieced
his flesh like a lance.

ISHMAEL
Although the ivory leg still
reminded entire, he did not deem
it trustworthy and ordered the
ship's carpenter to make another.

Lights up on the Carpenter working on an ivory leg. Ahab approaches him slowly.

CARPENTER
Drat the file, and drat the bone!

He sneezes.

CARPENTER
This wretched bone dust is...
    (sneezes)
Bless my soul, it won't let me speak!

AHAB
Hello, man-maker!

CARPENTER
Just in time, Sir. If the captain
pleases, I will now mark the
length. Let me measure, Sir.

The carpenter kneels to measure Ahab's ivory leg. Ahab picks up the carpenter's vise.

AHAB
Measured for a leg! Good! Well,
it's not the first time. This is a
cogent vise thou hast here,
carpenter. Let me feel its grip
once. So, so...it does pinch some.

CARPENTER
Careful, Sir. It will break bones.

AHAB
No, fear. I like to feel something in this slippery world that can hold.

CARPENTER
I suppose...

AHAB
While you're making my leg perhaps I should order up complete man after a desirable pattern. Fifty feet high in his socks. Brass forehead with a quarter acre of fine brains. No heart though. No heart at all.

The carpenter sneezes.

AHAB
The fellow's impious! What are thou sneezing about?

CARPENTER
Bone is rather dusty, Sir.

AHAB
Take the hint then. And when thou art dead, never bury your bones under living people's noses.

CARPENTER
I guess so...Yes...

AHAB
When I come to mount this leg thou makest, I shall nevertheless feel another leg in the same identical place with it. Canst thou not drive that old Adam away?

CARPENTER
I have heard, Sir...that a dismasted man never entirely loses the feeling of his old spar.

AHAB
If I still feel the smart of my crushed leg, though it be now so long dissolved...why shouldn't you feel the fiery pains of hell for ever, and without a body?

                    CARPENTER
          I ahh...I'm not quite sure...Sir.

                    AHAB
          Pudding heads should never grant
          premises.

                    CARPENTER
          I'm not a thinker, captain. I just
          do my job and work away.

                    AHAB
          But even you must feel the power of
          the white whale...tempting us...
          leading us forward.

                    CARPENTER
          That's Moby Dick, right? They've
          been talking about him down in the
          forecastle. Said you'd give that
          gold doubloon on the mast to the
          first man who spies him.

                    AHAB
          I will destroy the creature.

                    CARPENTER
          Yes. Of course. Lots of oil in a
          whale that size.

Ahab approaches the carpenter.

                    AHAB
          With your vise, you force the wood
          to bend a new direction. With my
          own will, I'll make you...even
          you...know my purpose.

                    CARPENTER
          I'd rather not, Captain if...

                    AHAB
          Do you see my leg? It was Moby Dick
          that did this to me.

                    CARPENTER
          Yes, but...

                    AHAB
          He's wounded others...killed others
          ...don't you feel a duty to avenge
          that suffering?

                    CARPENTER
          I just do my job, sir.

                    AHAB
          The whale tasks me. He heaps me. I
          see in him outrageous strength,
          with an inscrutable malice sinewing
          it. That inscrutable thing is
          chiefly what I hate and I will
          wreak my hate upon him.

                    CARPENTER
          I...just do my job.

Ahab gives up and walks away.

                    AHAB
          Then do it. How long before the new
          leg is done?

                    CARPENTER
          Perhaps an hour.

                    AHAB
          Bungle a way at it then, and bring
          it to me.

Blackout on the carpenter.

                    AHAB
          Here I am, proud as a Greek god,
          and yet standing debtor to this
          blockhead for a bone to stand on.
          Away with all flesh. I'll get a
          crucible, and into it, and dissolve
          myself down to one small compendious
          vertebra. So.

The lights change. Carrying tattered banners, the three
harpooners run across the stage. Members of the crew rattle a
piece of sheet metal that gives a thundering sound. They play
tribal instruments: drums, gourds, and wooden flutes.

                    QUEEQUEG
          The wind grew stronger. The air
          became heavy and moist. And suddenly...

                    TASHTEGO
          A typhoon burst from the cloudless
          sky, like an exploding bomb upon a
          sleeping town.

                    DAGGOO
          When darkness came on, sky and sea
          roared and split with the thunder,
          and blazed with the lightning that
          showed the disabled sails fluttering
          like rags.

Starbuck approaches Ahab.

> **STARBUCK**
> We must send down the main-top-sail, Sir. The band is working loose. Shall I strike it, Sir?

> **AHAB**
> Strike nothing. Lash it. If I had sky-sail poles, I'd sway them up now.

> **STARBUCK**
> God is against thee, old man. Let me square the yards while we may and make a fair wind of it homewards.

> **AHAB**
> You are bound to me, Starbuck. And I am bound to my oath with heart, soul and body...lungs and life.

> **STARBUCK**
> Sir...

> **AHAB**
> Strike nothing, and stir nothing, but lash everything! Quick, and see to it!

Ahab exits. Sound of thunder. Stubb and Flask sway back and forth on ropes.

> **FLASK**
> You change like the wind, Stubb. Gusting one way...then the other.

> **STUBB**
> Me? Stubb? I'm as steady as the sun.

> **FLASK**
> Only yesterday, you said that any ship Ahab sails in should carry something extra on its insurance policy...just as though it was loaded with gun powder. Stop, now. Didn't you say so?

> **STUBB**
> Well, suppose I did. What then? I've part changed my flesh since that time, why not my mind?

> **FLASK**
> You said this voyage was dangerous. And now you want to give up our lightning rods.

Thunder. They cling to the ropes.

> **STUBB**
> Who worries about lightning? I suppose you want every man in the world to go about with a small lightning rod running up the corner of his hat. Is that what you want? Is it? Be sensible, Flask. Why don't you be sensible?

> **FLASK**
> It's too wet to be sensible.

Stubb swings wildly on the rope.

> **STUBB**
> Lord, Lord, that the winds that come from heaven should be so unmannerly! This is a nasty night, lad.

Thunder. Starbuck crosses the deck.

> **STUBB**
> Oh! Jolly is the gale,
> And a joker is the whale,
> A' flourishin' his tail ---
> Such a funny, sporty, gamy, jesty, joky, hoky-poky lad, is the Ocean!

> **STARBUCK**
> Let the typhoon sing, Mr. Stubb! If thou art a brave man, thou wilt hold thy peace.

> **STUBB**
> But I am not a brave man. Never said I was a brave man. I'm a coward and I sing to keep up my spirits.

> **STARBUCK**
> Madman! Look through my eyes if thou hast none of thine own.

Stubb slides down the rope and approaches Starbuck.

> **STUBB**
> What! How can you see better of a dark night that anybody else?

Starbuck grabs Stubb by the shoulder and points downstage.

                    STARBUCK
          Here! See that the gale comes from
          the eastward, the very course Ahab
          is to run for Moby Dick? The very
          course he swung to this day noon!

Starbuck lets go of Stubb and steps away.

                    STUBB
          I don't half understand you. What's
          in the wind?

                    STARBUCK
          If we turn the ship, the gale that
          now hammers us will drive us
          towards home. To windward, all is
          blackness of doom. But look
          homeward...the sky lightens.

Thunder. The banners are whipping through the air.

                    STARBUCK
          The rods! The lightning rods!
          Throw their chains overboard!
          Quick!

Ahab steps from the shadows. Fedallah stands beside him.

                    AHAB
          Forget the rods. Let's have fair
          play here, though we be the weaker
          side. Let them be, sir.

                    STARBUCK
          Look aloft! The Saint Elmo's lights!

A orange light glows from the tip of the mast. The three
harpooners stand on the skeleton.

                    DAGGOO
          Daggoo loomed up to thrice his real
          stature, and seemed the black cloud
          from which the thunder had come.

                    TASHTEGO
          Tashtego's shark-white teeth
          strangely gleamed...

                    QUEEQUEG
          While Queequeg's tattooing burned
          like Satanic blue flame on his body.

The orange light fades. Starbuck approaches Stubb.

STARBUCK
What do you think now, Mr. Stubb? I
don't hear you singing.

STUBB
(frightened)
Perhaps, it's a sign of good luck.
Yes, good luck. For those masts are
rooted in a hold that is going to
be filled with sperm-oil and the
oil will work up into the masts
like candles and...and...

Thunder. Light appears on the mast.

STUBB
Mercy on us all!

AHAB
Aye! Look at it. Mark it well. The
flame but lights the way to the
White Whale!

Blackout. Spotlight on Ahab. He presses a hand on his eyes.

AHAB
The lightning flashes through my
skull. My eyeballs ache. My whole
beaten brain seems as beheaded, and
rolling on some stunning ground.
Light though thou be, thou leapest
out of darkness. But I am darkness
leaping out of light.

He opens up his eyes and stares at the spotlight.

AHAB
Oh, thou foundling fire! Here again
with haughty agony, I read my
origin. I leap with thee. I burn
with thee. I worship thee.

Blackout. Ahab exits. Lights up slowly. Ishmael stands in the crow's nest while the crew work at various tasks.

ISHMAEL
The next morning, the not-yet-
subsided sea rolled in long slow
billows of mighty bulk, pushing her
on like giants' palms outspread.

Starbuck, Stubb and Flask walk past the carpenter.

> STUBB
> We could have lost a man during that storm. One wave...and you'd be over the side.

> FLASK
> With no life-buoy to save you.

> STUBB
> I don't want to drown at sea. I really don't. Only the white caps come to your funeral.

> FLASK
> And no life-buoy.

> STARBUCK
> What of it? Perhaps the ship's owners wished us to trust in God's mercy.

> FLASK
> I'll take his mercy...and a life-buoy.

Queequeg approaches the men and gestures to Starbuck.

> STARBUCK
> Yes. What is it?

> QUEEQUEG
> (gestures to coffin)
> Life...

> STARBUCK
> A life-buoy of a coffin?

> STUBB
> That's a peculiar idea.

> FLASK
> No, it's a good idea. Carpenter!

The Carpenter shuffles over to them.

> FLASK
> Make us a life-buoy. You can use this.

> CARPENTER
> Mr. Starbuck...I...

> STARBUCK
> There's nothing else for it. Rig it up, carpenter. That's an order.

CARPENTER
Shall I nail down the lid, sir?

STARBUCK
Aye.

CARPENTER
And shall I caulk the seams, sir?

STARBUCK
That's right.

CARPENTER
Speaking frankly, sir, I don't like this cobbling sort of business. First, I make a coffin...now, it's supposed to be a life-buoy. The whole thing's undignified. I like clean, virgin, fair-and-square mathematical jobs, something that regularly begins at the beginning, and is at the middle when midway, and comes to an end at the conclusion. It's the old woman's tricks to be giving cobbling jobs. Lord! What an affection all old women have for tinkers. I know an old woman of sixty-five who ran away with a bald-headed young tinker and...

STARBUCK
That's enough, carpenter.

STUBB
More than enough. Words leak out of him like oil in a rotten barrel.

STARBUCK
Start the work...right away.

The three men cross the deck while the carpenter continues muttering.

CARPENTER
And that's the reason I never would work for lonely old widows ashore. They might have taken it in their heads to...

Ahab appears on deck. He looks up at Ishmael.

AHAB
You! In the crow's nest! In which direction are we sailing?

                    ISHMAEL
          East-south-east, Sir.

                    AHAB
          Thou liest! Heading East at this hour
          in the morning, and the sun astern?

Ahab walks over to the compass mounted at the base of the
mast.

                    STARBUCK
          We are following the compass, Sir.

                    AHAB
          The compass points east, but we're
          going west. I have it! It has happened
          before. Last night's thunder turned
          our compasses...that's all.
                    (to Starbuck)
          Thou hast heard of such a thing, I
          take it?

                    STARBUCK
          Aye. But it has never happened to
          me, Sir.

                    AHAB
          Mr. Stubb...bring me an iron lance,
          a top-maul, and the smallest of the
          sail-makers needles. Quick!

Stubb hurries away.

                    AHAB
          When a ship is hit by lightning, the
          compass can lose its lodestone virtue.
                    (to the crew)
          Men! The thunder has turned old
          Ahab's needles, but no matter. With
          a bit of iron, I can make a needle
          that will point as true as any.

Stubb returns with the materials. Ahab takes the needle and
the hammer.

                    AHAB
          Hold the lance upright without
          touching the deck.

He places the needle endwise on the base of the iron lance
and hammers it as Pip appears on deck.

                    PIP
          Captain Ahab! Sir! Pip's missing!
          Pip jumped from the whale-boat.

              STUBB
     Peace, thou crazy loon! Away from
     the quarter deck!

              PIP
     Sir, Sir! Here's Pip! Trying to get
     on board again!

              STUBB
     I ordered you away! Go or you'll
     feel a lash on your back!

              AHAB
     You pledge the lash quite easily,
     Mr. Stubb. As it you were calling
     for a cup of rum.

              STUBB
     The boy should stay in the crew's
     quarters. I've told him this.
     Starbuck, too.

              AHAB
     The boy should have stayed in your boat.

              STUBB
     It's not my fault, Captain. No
     one's to blame.

Ahab approaches Pip.

              AHAB
     The greater idiot ever scolds the
     lesser.
              (stares at Pip)
     Who are you, boy? I see not my
     reflection in the vacant pupils of
     your eyes. Oh God! That man should
     be a thing for immortal souls to
     sieve through! Who are you, boy?
     Tell me...

              PIP
     Bell-boy, Sir. Steward. Ship's
     crier. Ding, dong, ding! Pip! Pip!
     Pip! One hundred pounds of clay
     reward for Pip. Five feet high.
     Looks cowardly. Ding, dong, ding!
     Who's seen Pip the coward!

              AHAB
     Oh, ye frozen heavens. You did
     beget this luckless child, and have
     abandoned him.

                    STUBB
          Sir, let me send him back to the
          crew's quarters.

                    AHAB
          No. I'll send him to my own cabin.
                    (to Pip)
          You touch my inmost center, boy.
          You are tied to me by cords woven
          of my heart-strings.
                    (holds out needle)
          Take this, Starbuck. The compass
          will obey my command.

                    ISHMAEL
          Ship approaching, Sir. On the
          leeward side!

A sailor leads Pip away. Captain Gardiner appears on platform that designates another ship.

                    TASHTEGO
          A ship called The Rachel, bore
          directly down upon the Pequod, all
          her spars thickly clustering with men.

                    DAGGOO
          At the time, the Pequod was making
          good speed through the water, but
          as the stranger drew close to her...

                    QUEEQUEG
          The ship's sails all fell together
          and life fled from the smitten hull.

                    STUBB
                    (to Flask)
          Bad news. She brings bad news. I
          feel it.

                    AHAB
                    (to the Captain)
          Hello! Hast thou seen the White Whale?

                    CAPTAIN GARDINER
          Aye, yesterday. Have you seen a
          whale-boat adrift?

                    AHAB
          No. Nothing. Let me come aboard. I
          must talk to you.

Captain Gardiner walks from the platform to the stage.

CAPTAIN GARDINER
No. I will come to your ship.

AHAB
Mr. Stubb! Flask! Give assistance!

The two men help Captain Taylor onto the Pequod's deck.

CAPTAIN GARDINER
Hello, Captain Ahab. I didn't know you were in these water. I'm Captain Gardiner...also from Nantucket.

AHAB
I know who you are. Tell me, where is the whale? Not killed...was he? Not killed!

CAPTAIN GARDINER
No.

AHAB
What happened? How was it?

CAPTAIN GARDINER
Late yesterday afternoon, three of my boats engaged a shoal of whales about five miles windward from the ship. As they chased them, a White Whale loomed out of the blue water and I sent my reserve boat after it.

AHAB
Yes. Go on.

CAPTAIN GARDINER
We couldn't...see. They were too far away. The sailor up in the crow's nest thought that they had fastened to the White Whale. He saw the diminished dotted boat and then a swift gleam of bubbling bright water, and after that...nothing more.

AHAB
They attached their lines to him and he ran away.

CAPTAIN GARDINER
Yes. It's common enough. We weren't alarmed...yet. The recall signals were placed on the rigging, then darkness came on and we sailed off in the opposite direction to pick up the three windward boats. That was my responsibility as a Captain. I have followed my responsibility.

AHAB
And the whale?

CAPTAIN GARDINER
When we had picked up the windward, we turned around and crowded on sail. I placed every other man aloft on the looked, lit a fire in the try-pots for a beacon. I lowered my spare boats and searched the area...dashed on and lowered my boats again...dashed on and found nothing.

AHAB
In which direction did the whale...

CAPTAIN GARDINER
The boat is still lost! I need your help, Captain Ahab. Together, we can search the whole area...sailing four or five miles apart on parallel lines.

AHAB
I have my own duty, Captain Gardiner.

CAPTAIN GARDINER
My boy, my own boy is on the last boat! He's a little lad...but twelve-years-old. I brought him on this voyage to teach him our vocation. I didn't think that...

AHAB
I'm sorry, Captain. I can't help.

CAPTAIN GARDINER
I'll pay you if there be no other way! For 48 hours let me charter your ship...for 48 hours only... only that...you must, oh, you must, and you <u>shall</u> do this thing.

Ahab turns and walks away from Gardiner.

                    CAPTAIN GARDINER
        I will not go till you say _aye_ to
        me. Do to me as you would have me
        do to you in the like case. For
        you too have a boy, Captain Ahab...
        a child of your old age...nestling
        safely at home.

Ahab stops walking.

                    CAPTAIN GARDINER
        Yes, yes, you relent. I see it.
            (to the crew)
        Run, run, men, now, and and stand
        by to square the yards.

Ahab turns and faces Gardiner.

                    AHAB
        Avast! Touch not a rope-yarn!
            (approaches Gardiner)
        Captain Gardiner, I will not do it.
        Even now I lose time. Goodbye,
        goodbye. God bless you, man, and
        may I forgive myself, but I must go.
            (walks away)
        Mr. Starbuck, look at the binnacle
        watch, and in three minutes from
        this present instant warn off all
        strangers. Then brace forward
        again, and let the ship sail as
        before.

Ahab exits. Starbuck approaches Gardiner.

                    STARBUCK
        I'm sorry, Captain. I...

                    CAPTAIN GARDINER
        Have pity for your own souls.

Captain Gardiner exits. The light begins to fade. Clinging to ropes, the three harpooners look downstage at the other ship.

                    TASHTEGO
        Soon the two ships diverged their
        wakes. And long as the Rachel was
        in view, she was seen to yaw towards
        every dark spot, however small, on
        the sea.

                    QUEEQUEG
          The ship cut against the waves,
          weeping with spray, but still
          remained without comfort.

                    DAGGOO
          She was Rachel, weeping for her
          children, because they were not.

Music. The carpenter kneels beside the coffin and begins to
turn it into a life-buoy.

                    CARPENTER
          Tap! Tap! Let me see. Nail down the
          lid. Caulk the seams. Hang it with
          the snap-spring over the ship's
          stern. Tap! Tap! Let's see...how
          many in the ship's company, all
          told? But I've forgotten. Anyway,
          I'll have me thirty separate life-
          lines, each three-feet long hanging
          all round to the coffin. Then, if
          the hull go down, there be thirty
          lively fellows all fighting for one
          coffin, a sign not seen very often
          beneath the sun! Tap! Tap! Come
          hammer, caulking-iron, pitch-pot,
          and marling-spike! Let's do it!

Light on Ahab watching the carpenter. Pip stands beside him.

                    AHAB
          There's a sight. There's a sound.
          The gray-headed woodpecker tapping
          the hollow tree. Blind and dumb
          might well be envied now. A most
          malicious wag, that fellow. Rat-
          tat! So man's seconds tick.

Ahab walks through the ribs of the whale, entering his cabin.
Pip follows him.

                    PIP
          Where are you going, sir? And can I
          follow?

                    AHAB
          No, lad. You must not follow Ahab
          now. There is something in you
          which I feel too curing to my
          malady. Like cures like. And for
          this hunt, my sickness becomes my
          most desired health. Stay here...
          and sit in my chair...and they will
          serve you as if you were the captain.

PIP
They tell me, sir, that Stubb did once desert poor little Pip, whose drowned bones now show white. But I will never desert you, sir, as Stubb did him.

AHAB
I tell you no. It can not be.

Ahab turns to go and Pip follows him.

PIP
Good master!

AHAB
Beware. For Ahab too is mad. Listen, and you will often hear my ivory foot upon the deck, and still know that I am there. And now I quit thee. God forever bless thee... and save thee...if it come to that.

Ahab walks out of the cabin.

PIP
Here he this instant stood. I stand in his air. But I'm alone. Now were even poor Pip here I could endure it, but he's missing. Pip! Pip! Ding, dong, ding! Who's seen Pip? A little lad, five-feet high, hang-dog look, and cowardly! Jumped from a whale-boat once. Seen him? No! Well, then, fill up again, captains, and let's drink shame upon all cowards! I name no names.
      (sits on chair)
I'll stay here. Yes. Although this stern strikes rocks and they bulge through and oysters come to join me.

Blackout on Pip. Lights up as Ahab as he takes his harpoon and crosses the deck. Stubb is up in the crow's nest.

AHAB
What d'ye see, Mr. Stubb? Sharp! Sharp! Any sign of the White Whale?

STUBB
No, Sir.

AHAB
You would sing out if you saw it?

                    STUBB
          Of course, Captain.

Ahab turns to Starbuck.

                    AHAB
          And you, Mr. Starbuck. What would
          you do?

                    STARBUCK
          I would...follow orders, Sir.

                    AHAB
          Such are the various categories of
          humanity...those who take orders,
          those who give orders, and those
          who do nothing at all.

                    STUBB
          Ship approaching on the starboard side!

Light on the platform. Dressed in rags, the Captain of the
Delight and a sailor finish sewing a dead man into his hammock.

                    DAGGOO
          Another ship, most miserably
          misnamed "The Delight" drew near.

                    TASHTEGO
          On the shears above the quarter-
          deck lay the shattered, white ribs
          and splintered planks of what had
          once been a whale-boat.

                    QUEEQUEG
          But now you saw through this wreck,
          as plainly as you see through the
          peeled and bleaching skeleton of a
          horse.

                    AHAB
          Have you seen the whale?

Startled, the Captain of the Rachel stands and faces Ahab.
The lights fade except for spots on Ishmael and the two
Captains.

                    CAPTAIN OF THE DELIGHT
          Have we "seen" him?
                    (points upward)
          What hangs on the shears was once a
          whaling boat.
                    (looks down)
          This was once a man.

> AHAB
> Did you kill the whale?

> CAPTAIN OF THE DELIGHT
> The harpoon is not yet forged that will ever do that.

Ahab raises his harpoon.

> AHAB
> Look ye...here in this hand I hold his death.

> CAPTAIN OF THE DELIGHT
> Then God keep thee, old man. See'st that I bury but one of five stout men, who were alive only yesterday...but were dead before night. Only this one I bury. The rest were buried before they died. You sail upon their tomb.
> (turns to sailor)
> Are ye ready there? Place the plank then on the rail, and lift the body. So, then...

The sailor carries the wrapped body up the aisle.

> CAPTAIN OF THE DELIGHT
> May the resurrection and the life...

> AHAB
> Brace forward! Up helm!

Blackout on Ahab.

> ISHMAEL
> But the suddenly started Pequod was not quick enough to escape the splash that the corpse made as it struck the side. And...as our ship glided by...the other Captain saw the strange life-buoy hanging at our stern.

Blackout on Ishmael.

> CAPTAIN OF THE DELIGHT
> Ha! Yonder! Look yonder, men! In vain they fly from our sad burial. They turn their taffrail and show us a coffin!

Blackout on the Captain. The lights slowly rise as Queequeg climbs to the top of the skeleton.

                QUEEQUEG
The next day dawned with a clear
and steel-blue sky. The pensive air
was transparently pure and soft...

Ahab walks across the deck ard gazes out at the sea.

                DAGGOO
And the sea heaved with long,
strong, lingering swells.

                TASHTEGO
Above, glided the snow-white wings
of small, unspeckled birds. At that
fair moment, the firmaments of air
and sea seemed one.

Ahab turns and sees Starbuck.

                AHAB
Starbuck...

                STARBUCK
Captain?

                AHAB
It is...a mild, mild wind, and a
mild looking sky.

                STARBUCK
Yes. This sky reminds me of home.

                AHAB
On such a day, at the age of
eighteen, I struck my first whale
and...as a fatherless son...
received the praise of my captain.
That was forty...forty years ago.

                STARBUCK
I also remember the first time I
killed a whale. I was wet and tired
and full of pride.

                AHAB
Pride. Yes. That is the sin that
leads to all others. I was proud of
my skill and bravery and so for
forty years I have not spent three
ashore. I didn't know...I only
half-suspected...how for forty
years I would feed on dry salted
fare when even the poorest landsman
has fresh fruit to his daily hand.

STARBUCK
I'm sure that your child misses
you. And your wife.

AHAB
Wife? A wife? Rather a widow with
her husband alive. Aye, I widowed
that poor girl when I married her.
  (turns away)
And then, the madness and the frenzy,
the boiling blood and the smoking
brow. For a thousand lowerings, I
have chased my prey...more a demon
than a man. I feel deadly faint,
bowed, and humped, as though I
were Adam, staggering beneath the
piled centuries since Paradise.

He turns and faces Starbuck.

AHAB
Close! Stand close to me, Starbuck.
Let me look into your eyes. This is
better than to gaze into sea or
sky...better than to gaze upon God.
This is a magic glass, man. I see
my wife and my child in your eyes.

STARBUCK
Captain, let us leave these deadly
waters. Let us home. I have a wife
and child, too.

AHAB
About this time, my boy wakes from
his noon nap, sits up in bed, and
his mother tells him how I am
abroad upon the deep, but will yet
come back to dance him again.

STARBUCK
Yes! We are the same! My Mary
promised our boy that, every
morning, he would be carried to the
hill to catch the first glimpse of
his father's sail. Yes! We'll do
it! We'll head for home!

Ahab turns and sees Fedallah watching him.

AHAB
  No.

                    STARBUCK
          Come, Captain, study out the
          course, and let us away.

                    AHAB
          No.

                    STARBUCK
          See! Your boy is at the window.
          Mine is standing on the hill.

                    AHAB
          No! I can not!

Ahab turns away. Starbuck exits.

                    AHAB
          What is it? What hidden lord and
          master commands me against all
          natural longings? Is it my own
          desire or another's that lifts this
          arm? We are turned round and round
          in this world like yonder windlass,
          and Fate is the handspike.

Within the skeleton of the whale, Pip strikes a large drum.
A few sailors lie in their hammocks while Ahab crosses the
deck.

                    QUEEQUEG
          At daybreak, a long slick appeared
          on the sea ahead.

                    TASHTEGO
          It was as smooth as oil...and
          resembled the polished surface at
          the mouth of a deep, rapid stream.

                    AHAB
          Man the mast-heads! Daggoo, call
          all hands! Mr. Starbuck, help raise
          me up!

Daggoo pounds on the deck with two handspikes. The sailors
roll out of their hammocks and scramble to the top of the
skeleton while Tashtego climbs the mast.

Ahab slips his good leg into the block and tackle arrangement
fastened to the mast and Starbuck raises him off the deck.

                    AHAB
          What d'ye see? Sing out!

                    THE CREW
          Nothing! Nothing, sir!

                    AHAB
          Men on the gallant sails! Stunsails!
          Alow and aloft, and on both sides!

Sound of the drum. Ahab hangs above the deck.

                    AHAB
          There...There...A hump like a snow
          hill and...there she blows! It's
          Moby Dick!

                    TASHTEGO (simultaneous)
          There she blows!

                    AHAB
          There she blows! There again! There
          again! He's going to sound! In the
          stunsails! Down top-gallant-sails!
          Lower me, Mr. Starbuck. Lower.
          Lower. Quick. Quicker!

Starbuck lowers Ahab back onto the deck. The crew places the three benches --- the whale boats --- into position. Ishmael joins Stubb's crew.

                    AHAB
          Helm there! Luff, luff a point!
          Steady, man steady! There go the
          flukes! No, it's only black water.
          All ready the boats! Mr. Starbuck,
          stay on board when I give chase to
          Moby Dick. That hazard shall not be
          yours.

Ahab crosses the deck to his whale boat.

                    STUBB
          He is heading straight to leeward,
          Sir. Right away from us. He can't
          have seen the ship yet.

                    AHAB
          Stand by the braces! Hard down the
          helm! Boats! Boats! Now!

Lights on the crews of the three whale boats. (Note: a large white strip of cloth has been attached to the mast rope. The rolled-up cloth is placed beneath Ahab's boat).

                    TASHTEGO
          Like noiseless nautilus shells, the
          three whale boats sped through the sea.

                    QUEEQUEG
          As they neared the whale, the ocean
          grew still more smooth...like a
          noon-meadow.

                    DAGGOO
          At length, the hunters came so
          close they saw the whale's white
          hump sliding along the sea.

                    AHAB
          Look! There's a shattered lance in
          his back!

                    TASHTEGO
          The sea birds skimmed like a
          canopy over the fish while a few
          perched on this broken pole, their
          long tail feathers streaming like
          pennons.

                    STUBB
          Closer, boys. Closer...Closer...

                    FLASK
          Watch the Captain. Wait for him to
          throw his lance...

Ahab raises his harpoon.

                    AHAB
          Ready? Stand ready. He's sounding!

                    DAGGOO
          The whale's fore-part slowly rose
          from the water...and for instant
          his whole marbleized body formed a
          high arch...until he sounded and
          went out of sight.

                    AHAB
          He'll stay down for an hour. Mr.
          Flask, go bring up the ship.

                    FLASK
          Yes, Sir.

                    STUBB
          The birds, Captain! Look at the
          birds!

Sound of the drum. Ahab looks down at the sea.

                    TASHTEGO
          The birds flew towards Ahab's boat
          and fluttered over the water there.
          And Ahab peered down into the
          depths and saw a white living spot
          no bigger than a white weasel,
          rising up...rising...and then there
          was plainly revealed two long
          crooked rows of white, glistening
          teeth. It was Moby Dick's open
          mouth...yawning beneath the boat
          like an open-doored marble tomb.

                    AHAB
          Hold your oars! Stand by to stern!

Starbuck and Queequeg pull on the mast rope. The large white
fabric slithers from beneath Ahab's boat, then billows above
the stage.

                    QUEEQUEG
          The whale shot his pleated head
          lengthwise beneath Ahab's boat...

                    TASHTEGO
          And took the bows within his
          mouth and shook the slight cedar
          as a cruel cat her mouse.

                    DAGGOO
          The frail gunwales bent in,
          collapsed and snapped, as both
          jaws, like enormous shears, bit the
          craft in twain.

Blackout. The white fabric falls to the stage. Spotlight on
Ahab.

                    AHAB
          Moby Dick circled around the
          wrecked crew and then...swam off.
          And disappeared.

Lights up. Men shout and hurry across the deck as the three
whaling crews return to the ship. Starbuck helps the
exhausted Ahab. Flask climbs to the crow's nest.

                    STARBUCK
          Are you all right, Captain. Can I...

                    AHAB
          My boat's harpoon? Is it safe?

Stubb steps forward with Ahab's harpoon.

STUBB
Aye, Sir. For it was not darted. This is it.

AHAB
Give it to me Any missing men?

STARBUCK
All accounted for.

AHAB
Good. That's good.
   (turns away)
Can you see the whale? Whose doubloon is now? D'ye see him?

FLASK
He continued straight to leeward, Sir. There's nothing left but the ruins of your boat.

STUBB
I guess he didn't like it, Captain. Like a thistle in the mouth of an ass...it pricked him too keenly.

AHAB
Groan...not laugh...should be heard before a wreck, Mr. Stubb. Did I not know you were as brave as fearless fire...and as mechanical... I would swear you were a poltroon.

STARBUCK
Aye, Sir. A wrecked boat is a solemn sight. A bad omen.

Ahab shakes his head and walks towards the mast.

AHAB
Omen? Omen? If the gods think to speak outright to man, they will honorably speak outright...not shake their heads and give an old You two are the opposite poles of one thing. Starbuck is Stubb reversed, and Stubb is Starbuck, and you two are all mankind. Ahab stands alone among the millions of the peopled earth, nor gods nor men his neighbors.
   (pauses)
Cold. Cold. I shiver. How now, Mr. Flask. Still no sign of the whale?

FLASK
Can't see anything, Sir. Too dark.

AHAB
We'll continue leeward, but slowly. Down royals and top-gallant sails, Mr. Starbuck. We must not run over him before morning.
    (touches the doubloon)
Men, this gold is mine, for I earned it. But I shall let it abide here till the White Whale is dead. I'll give it to whoever first raises him on the day he's killed. If I see him first, ten times its sum shall be divided among you.
    (to Starbuck)
Away, now. The deck is yours, Sir.

Music. The lights fade.

ISHMAEL
The ship tore on, leaving such a furrow in the sea as when a cannon-ball, missent, becomes a ploughshare and turns up the level field.

Spotlight on Ahab as he approaches Fedallah.

AHAB
For months, you have been my shadow and now you abandon me.
    (no response)
Speak, Fedallah. I order you to speak. Three years ago, I found you clinging to some wreckage on the open sea. I pulled you from the water. Fed you. Kept you on this ship. We are two spirits sharing the same life.

FEDALLAH
I will not leave you, Captain. Not yet.

AHAB
"Not yet?" That means you will go.

FEDALLAH
I shall go before you...as your pilot...and then see you again.

AHAB
No riddles, Fedallah. You know the future. I'm sure of it. When will I die? Tell me that secret.

                    FEDALLAH
          I will go in one coffin and be
          followed by another.

                    AHAB
          A second coffin. Yes. Is that mine?

                    FEDALLAH
          No coffin or hearse can carry your
          body. And only hemp can kill you.

                    AHAB
          Riddles twisting into more riddles.
          And the truth is like a child lost
          in a dark cave. Tell me. Speak. Will
          the white whale die?

                    FEDALLAH
          First light, Captain. You men are
          calling you.

Music. Lights up. Men climb the ropes and stand in the crow's nest while Ahab paces across the deck.

                    AHAB
          Do you see him? See anything?

                    STARBUCK
          Nothing, Sir.

                    AHAB
          Turn up all hands and make sail.

                    STARBUCK
          Daggoo...

Daggoo pounds on the deck with two handspikes. A few sailors roll out of their hammocks.

                    AHAB
          The whale travels faster than I
          thought. Raise the top-gallant sails.

                    STARBUCK
          Up the top-gallant! Trim the main!

                    AHAB
          Aye, they should have been kept on
          her all night. But no matter. 'Tis
          but resting for the rush.

Stubb climbs one of the ropes.

> **STUBB**
> By salt and hemp, but this swift motion of the deck creeps up one's legs and tingles at the heart. Ha! Ha! This ship and I are two brave fellows! Someone take me up, and launch me, spine-wise, on the sea!

> **TASHTEGO**
> There she blows! Right ahead!

> **STUBB**
> Aye, aye! I knew it! He can't escape! Blow on and split your spout! Blister your lungs!

Ahab moves downstage and looks out at the sea.

> **AHAB**
> Where is he?

> **FLASK**
> Can't see him now, Sir.

> **AHAB**
> You have been deceived, men. It's not the whale. Moby Dick would not cast one odd jet, then disappear...

> **QUEEQUEG**
> The ship continued leeward. All the spars in full bearing of mortals, ready and ripe for their fate.

> **AHAB**
> There...There...

> **TASHTEGO**
> A mile away, the whale breached from the sea...rising up with utmost velocity from the depths and into the air...

> **DAGGOO**
> Then falling back down into a mountain of dazzling foam.

> **THE CREW**
> There she breaches! The White Whale!

> **AHAB**
> Aye, breach your last to the sun, Moby Dick! Thy hour and thy harpoon are at hand!
> (MORE)

                    AHAB
               (to the crew)
          Down! Down all of you, but one man
          to the fore. The boats! Stand by!

The crew slide down the ropes and assemble in the three
whaling boats.

                    STARBUCK
          Let us wait and...

                    AHAB
          Wait? Wait for damnation! Mr. Starbuck,
          the ship is thine. Keep away from
          the boats, but keep near them.

Ahab reaches his whaling boat.

                    AHAB
          Lower away! Lower, all!

Lights on the three whaling boats. Pip beats the drum.
Starbuck and Queequeg pull the mast rope and the white fabric
rises into the air --- billowing like a huge ghost behind the
three whaling boats.

                    ISHMAEL
          The three boats cut through the
          waves as Moby Dick turned, and came
          directly for them.

                    AHAB
          Pull! Pull hard! We'll take the
          whale head-to-head!

                    STUBB
          He wants to taste our iron, boys!
          Let's help the fellow!

                    FLASK
          Ready! Get ready!

Three men -- the Manila sailor, Ishmael, and a sailor --
move away from the benches and stand slightly outside the
three patches of light.

Each man holds a rope. The Manila sailor is attached to Ahab.
Ishmael is attached to Stubb. The sailor is attached to Flask.

                    AHAB
          Now!

Ahab throws his harpoon. The other two boats join the attack.
The men crisscross back and forth --- showing the confusion
of harpoon lines.

                    TASHTEGO
          The White Whale rushed among the
          boats with open jaws, and a lashing
          tail...heedless of the irons darted
          at him from every boat.

                    STUBB
          Pull your oars! Harder! I see his
          blood!

                    DAGGOO
          He crossed and recrossed, and in a
          thousand ways entangled the slack
          of the three lines now fast to him
          ...pulling the devoted boats
          towards the planted irons.

Ahab tries avoid the rope.

                    AHAB
          Fedallah! Watch for the line!

The rope goes tight and touches Fedallah. He spins around and steps out of the light.

                    TASHTEGO
          Caught and twisted...corkscrewed in
          the mazes of line, loose harpoons
          and lances...the whale dragged the
          boats of Stubb and Flask towards
          his flukes and dashed them together.

                    STUBB
          Jump, men! Jump for your lives!

Blackout on Stubb and Flask. Lights remain on Queequeg and Ahab.

                    QUEEQUEG
          He dived down into the sea...
          disappearing into the boiling
          maelstrom...then rose back up and
          dashed his broad forehead against
          the bottom of Ahab's boat, and sent
          it, turning over and over into the air.

Pip stops beating the drum. Blackout on Ahab and Queequeg as the white fabric falls to the stage. Light on Ishmael sitting on the whale's skull.

ISHMAEL
The Pequod again bore down to the rescue and picked up the floating mariners, tubs, oars, and whatever else could be caught at, and safely landed them on her decks. There were sprained wrists and ankles, shattered oars and planks, inextricable intricacies of rope... all these were there.

Lights up as the crew returns to the ship. Ahab holds onto the Manila sailor.

AHAB
The leg is cracked...like a old tree touched by lightning.

STARBUCK
Carpenter! Get the carpenter!
    (to Ahab)
Here. Let me help you.

Starbuck helps Ahab over to a chair.

AHAB
Aye, Starbuck. 'Tis sweet to lean sometimes, be the leaner who he will. Would I have leaned oftener in my life.

Ahab sits down. The Carpenter approaches.

CARPENTER
Looks like the ferrule, Sir. I can't imagine why it cracked. I put good work in that leg.

STUBB
But no bones broken, Sir. I hope.

AHAB
Only this dead one, Stubb. D'ye see it? But even with a broken bone, old Ahab is untouched.
    (looks up)
Aloft there! Which way is the whale?

FLASK
Dead to leeward, Sir.

AHAB
Up helm, then. Pile on the sail again. Down the rest of the spare boats and rig them. Mr. Starbuck away...and muster the boat's crews.

Ahab tries to stand up.

                STARBUCK
    Let me first help thee towards the
    bulwarks, Sir.

The two men start to move across the deck.

                AHAB
    Oh, how this splinter gores me now.
    Accursed fate...that the captain in
    the soul should have such a craven mate.

                STARBUCK
    Sir?

                AHAB
    My body, man, not thee. Give me
    something for a cane. There. That
    shivered lance will do.

Stubb hands Ahab a broken harpoon.

                AHAB
    Where's Fedallah? The Parsee?

                STUBB
    I haven't...seen...

                AHAB
    Muster the men. Surely, he must
    have been picked up by the ship.

                STARBUCK
    All hands on deck!

The crew slides down the ropes to the deck. Ahab approaches the men.

                AHAB
    By heaven it cannot be! Missing?

                STUBB
    He must have been caught in...

                AHAB
    The black vomit wrench thee! Run all
    of you above and below, cabin and
    forecastle. Find him. Not gone. Not
    gone!

                STUBB
    Aye, Sir...caught among the tangles
    of your line. I thought I saw him
    dragging under.

                    AHAB
My line? Gone? Gone? What means
this little word? What death-knell
rings in it, that makes me shake as
if I were the belfry. Where's the
harpoon? Toss over the litter
there. Do you see it? No. No.
Blistered fool.
          (raises hand)
This hand did dart it. It's in the
fish.
          (to the crew)
Quick! All hands to the rigging of
the boats. Collect the oars. The
irons. Hoist the royals higher. Helm
there. Steady. Steady for your life!

                    STARBUCK
In Jesus' name, no more of this.
Two days chase. Twice stove to
splinters. Your evil shadow gone.
What more would you have? Shall we
keep chasing this murderous fish
till he kills the last man?

Ahab approaches Starbuck.

                    AHAB
Starbuck, of late I've felt strangely
moved to thee, but in this matter
of the whale, be the front of thy
face to me as the palm of this
hand...a lipless, unfeatured blank.
I'm the Fates' lieutenant. I act
under their orders as you must obey mine.
          (facing the crew)
Stand round me, men. You see an old
man leaning on a shivered lance,
propped up on a lonely foot. This
is my body's part, but my soul's a
centipede, that moves upon a
hundred legs. Do you believe in the
things called omens? Then laugh
aloud! For drowning things will
twice rise to the surface, then
sink for evermore. So with Moby
Dick. Two days he's floated.
Tomorrow, he'll rise once more,
but only to spout his last. Do you
feel brave, men? Brave?

                    THE CREW
Aye, Captain! Yes!

> STUBB
> As fearless fire!

He glances at Starbuck and walks away.

> AHAB
> Go. To your work. Up helm. A pull on all the sheets.

Blackout. Light on Ahab.

> AHAB
> The things called omens. Oh, how valiantly I seek to drive out of others' hearts what's clinched so fast in mine! Fedallah is gone. He told me that he was to die first, but that he would be seen again before I could perish. How's that? There's a riddle now might baffle all the lawyers backed by the ghosts of the whole line of judges. Like a hawk's beak it pecks my brain.

Blackout on Ahab. Light on the three harpooners.

> DAGGOO
> When the dusk descended, the whale was still in sight to leeward. So once more the sail was shortened, and everything passed nearly as on the previous night.

> TASHTEGO
> Only, the sound of hammers, and the hum of the grindstone was heard till nearly daylight, as the men rigged the spare boats and sharpened their fresh weapons for the morrow.

> QUEEQUEG
> Meanwhile, the carpenter made Ahab another leg while he stood in the scuttle and stared due eastward for the earliest sun.

Lights up. Sailors climb the ropes. Ahab and Starbuck cross the deck.

AHAB
We follow his infallible wake. The winds push us towards him. Out upon it! Were I the wind, I'd blow no more on such a wicked miserable world. I'd crawl somewhere to a cave, and slink there. And yet, these warm Trade Winds blow straight on and veer not from their mark...while something so unchangeable, and full as strong, blows my keeled soul along.
(looks at mast)
Aloft there! What do you see?

FLASK
Nothing, Sir!

AHAB
Nothing! And noon at hand! I've oversailed him. Aye, he's chasing me now. I might have known it. The harpoons he's towing slowed him down. We passed him in the darkness.
(to crew)
About! Come about!

STARBUCK
Come down! Everyone, but the lookouts! Man the boats!

The crew works quickly to arrange the whaling boats. Ahab looks out at the sea.

AHAB
Forehead to forehead, I meet him a third time. But let me have one more good look at the sea. There's a soft rain falling in the distance. It must lead somewhere...to something else than common land, more palmy than the palms.

STARBUCK
The boats are ready, Sir.

Ahab faces Starbuck.

AHAB
For the third time my soul's ship starts upon this voyage.

STARBUCK
Aye, sir. You will have it so.

                    AHAB
          Some ships sail from their ports,
          and ever afterwards are missing.

                    STARBUCK
          That's is the truth, Sir. The
          saddest truth.

                    AHAB
          Some men die at ebb tide. Some at
          the full of the flood. I feel now
          like a billow that's all one
          crested comb. Shake hands with me,
          man.

The two men shake hands.

                    STARBUCK
          Go not, Captain. Go...

Ahab pushes Starbuck's arm away and walks to his whale boat.
Ishmael joins Ahab's boat --- taking the place of the missing
Fedallah.

                    AHAB
          Lower away! Stand by the crew!

Pip calls from inside the skeleton.

                    PIP
          The sharks, Sir! Sharks!

Blackout. Lights on the three whale boats. Light on Starbuck.
Queequeg stands in the crow's-nest.

                    QUEEQUEG
          Scarce had Ahab pushed from the
          ship, when numbers of sharks,
          rising from out of the dark waters
          beneath the hull, maliciously
          snapped at the blades of the oars,
          every time they dipped in the water.

                    STARBUCK
          Oh, my God. What is this feeling
          that shoots through me, and leaves
          me so deadly calm, yet expectant...
          fixed at the top of a shudder.
          Thoughts of my wife fade into pale
          glories behind me. I seem to see my
          little boy's eyes grown wondrous
          blue.
                    (to Queequeg)
          You on the mast-head! Keep your eye
          upon the boats! Mark well the whale!

                    QUEEQUEG
          A sea-hawk appeared in the sky above
          the mast and began to tear at the
          red flag flying there.

                    STARBUCK
          He attacks with talons. Now, soars
          away. Where's the old man now?
          Let him see!

Blackout on Starbuck and Queequeg.

                    AHAB
          Hold your oars. The white whale has
          sounded. Stay still. We'll wait for
          him to rise...

                    DAGGOO
          Suddenly the waters around them
          slowly swell in broad circles, then
          quickly unheaved, as if sideways
          sliding from a submerged berg of ice.

                    TASHTEGO
          A low rumbling sound was heard, and
          the whale shot lengthwise from the
          sea...hovered for a moment in the
          rainbowed air, and then fell
          swamping back into the deep.

The white fabric rises into the air.

                    AHAB
          Give way! Give way on the oars!

                    DAGGOO
          The whale came churning his tail
          among the boats, and once more
          flailed them apart...dashing in one
          side of their upper bows.

                    STUBB
          Look at his back! See what he
          carries!

                    FLASK
          Remember the prophecy! That Ahab
          would meet Fedallah again!

Blackout on Stubb and Flask. Light on Fedallah as he twists
on a rope.

> ISHMAEL
> Lashed round and round to the
> fish's back was the half-torn body
> of the Parsee, his sable raiment
> frayed to shreds.

> AHAB
> Aye, I see you again. And Aye, you
> go before me.

Blackout on Fedallah.

> AHAB
> Stubb! Flask! Return to the ship.
> Repair the boats if you can in
> time.

The Manila sailor starts to rise.

> AHAB
> Down! I'll kill the first man that
> but offers to jump from this boat.
> You are not other men, but my arms
> and my legs, and so obey me!

Ahab looks at the ship.

> AHAB
> Tashtego! Nail a flag to the mast!
>   (to the crew)
> Now, pull! Pull on! All alive, now.
> We near him.

Lights on all members of the crew as they stand in their
final positions. Only Tashtego is moving --- climbing to the
top of the mast with a hammer and a red flag.

> ISHMAEL
> The craft ranged alongside the
> whale's flank and we were within
> the smoky mountain mist thrown off
> from his spout.

> AHAB
> Now! I meet thee!

Ahab jabs with his harpoon.

> ISHMAEL
> Moby Dick sideways writhed, then
> rolled his flank against our bow
> and darted through the weltering
> sea. Our line felt the strain and
> tug...then snapped in the empty air!

AHAB
What breaks in me? Some sinew cracks! Oars! Burst in upon him!

QUEEQUEG
Wheeling around, the whale caught sight of the nearing black hull of the ship.

DAGGOO
Seeing it as the source of all his persecutions...or bethinking it a larger and nobler foe...he bore down upon its advancing prow, smiting his jaws amid showers of foam.

AHAB
Oars! Slope downwards to thy depths! Dash on, my men! Will you not save my ship! Is that the second coffin? Is that it's fate?

Blackout on Ahab and his crew.

STARBUCK
The whale comes towards us! Up helm! Up helm! Is this the end of all my bursting prayers! Up helm again! My God, stand by me now!

Blackout on Starbuck.

STUBB
Stand not by me, but stand under me, whoever you are that will now help Stubb. Cherries! Cherries! Oh, Flask...of all the things in the world...I'd like one red cherry before we die!

FLASK
Cherries? I only wish that we were where they grow. The voyage is up.

Blackout on Stubb, Flask, and the other sailors.

QUEEQUEG
The solid buttress of the whale's forehead smote the ship's starboard bow, till men and timbers reeled. Through the breach, they heard the waters pour, as mountain torrents down a flume.

DAGGOO
Diving beneath the settling ship, the whale ran quivering along its keel, then shot to the surface within a few yards of Ahab's boat.

Lights up on Ahab. The white fabric is pushed forward and he stands alone in front of it. The fabric billows back and forth, almost overwhelming him.

AHAB
I turn my body from the sun. Oh, now I feel my topmost greatness lies in my topmost grief. Like a wave, I roll towards this all destroying creature. To the last, I grapple with thee. From hell's heart I stab at thee and...<u>thus</u>, I give up the spear.

Blackout on Ahab. The fabric falls to the stage. Only Pip and the three harpooners remain.

QUEEQUEG
The harpoon was darted. The stricken whale flew forward. With igniting velocity, the line ran through the groove...caught Ahab around the neck, and pulled him from the boat.

Blackout on Queequeg.

DAGGOO
The ship was pulled to the bottom while concentric circles seized Ahab's boat and all its crew...and spinning, animate and inanimate, all round and round in one vortex, ...while Tashtego nailed the flag to the subsiding spar.

Blackout on Daygoo. Tashtego hammers the flag to the top of the mast.

TASHTEGO
A sea-hawk now chanced to intercept its broad fluttering wing between the hammer and the wood and Tashtego, in his dead grasp, kept the hammer frozen there...as if Ahab's ship would not sink to hell till she dragged a living part of heaven with her.

Blackout on Tashtego.

          PIP
Now small fowls flew screaming over the yet yawning gulf...and the great shroud of the sea rolled on as it rolled five thousand years ago.

Blackout on Pip. Light on Ishmael.

          ISHMAEL
The drama's done. Then why do I step forth?

He walks towards the coffin.

          ISHMAEL
When the ship was destroyed, I was drawn towards the closing vortex, but when I reached it, it had subsided to a creamy pool. I floated there alone until the coffin life-buoy rose with great force from the ocean and fell beside me.

He sits on the coffin.

          ISHMAEL
Buoyed up by the coffin, for almost one whole day and night, I floated on the sea. The sharks glided by with padlocks on their mouths. The savage hawks sailed with sheathed beaks.

Captain Gardiner steps out of the darkness. He stares at Ishmael, then walks away.

          ISHMAEL
On the second day, a sail drew near, nearer, and picked me up at last. It was the Rachel...that in her retracing search after her missing children, only found another orphan.

Light on the three harpooners.

          QUEEQUEG
And god created great whales.

                    DAGGOO
          The great Leviathan that maketh the
          seas to seethe like a boiling pan.

                    TASHTEGO
          Hugest of living creatures, in the deep
          Stretched like a promontory, sleeps or swims
          And seems a moving land; and in his gills
          Draws in, and at his breath spouts out a sea.

Blackout on the three harpooners.

                    ISHMAEL
          And I alone am escaped to tell you
          my story.

Blackout.

THE PLAYWRIGHT

Mr. Lee is an award-winning playwright, novelist and poet who once worked a war correspondent for the *London Telegraph*. His plays have been produced by the Manhattan Theatre Club, Long Wharf Theatre, South Coast Repertory, the Bush Theater in London and a wide variety of other theatres.

Four of his produced plays can be found in *Plays of Love and Rage*.

Mr. Lee first read *Moby Dick* when he was twelve-years-old. He has read the novel countless times since then and was inspired to transform Herman Melville's masterpiece into a stage play.